Windows 7®
—No Problem!

Joli Ballew

A John Wiley & Sons, Ltd, Publication

ISBN 978-0-470-68967-7

A catalogue record for this book is available from the British Library

Set in 10.75pt ITC Berkeley Oldstyle Std and ITC Highlander Std, by Frog Box Design
Printed in the United States by RR Donnelley (Crawfordsville)

For mom, it's been over a year and I still think of you every day and miss you deeply.

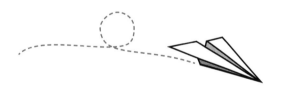

Contents

How to use this book   xv

This book is like a recipe   xvi

Active learning helps you remember   xvi

Link new knowledge to what you already know   xviii

    Make stronger links   xviii

Mysteries are memorable   xix

Why 'take a break' before the end of each chapter?   xx

Learn. Review. Repeat.   xxi

Review   xxi

1   Be more efficient with Windows 7   1

Make Windows 7 look more familiar   2

Work faster with Windows 7's new features   4

Access information quickly with gadgets   6

Manage multiple windows with Shake, Snap, and Peek   7

    Shake   8

    Snap   9

    Peek   10

Review   12

Experiment   13

2   Where's the e-mail program?   15

Windows Live Mail has to be downloaded? But I'm not online yet!   16

    Connect with Ethernet   16

    Connect to a wireless network   18

    Make notes for the next time you connect   20

Download and install Windows Live Mail   21

    Why sign up for a Windows Live ID?   22

    Set up Windows Live Mail   23

Get to know Windows Live Mail   30

    Explore the differences   32

What about spam?   34

Review   35

Experiment   36

Contents

3 Is surfing the Web the same as before?   **41**

Show the Menu Bar   42

Set multiple home pages to open automatically in tabs   44

Use Web Slices to access information that changes often   46

Get faster and better search results   48

   1. Add search providers   48

   2. Search using a specific provider   49

More information in fewer clicks   50

Review   54

Experiment   55

4 Manage your photos   **57**

Do you have Windows Live Photo Gallery?   58

Import pictures from a digital device   59

   Get the pictures off the device and onto the PC   60

Get pictures stored on other PCs   63

   Copy or move   63

   Use photos over a network   64

Get organized   66

Edit your pictures   68

Share your photos   69

Review   71

Experiment   72

5 Windows Media Player   **75**

Access music on other PCs   76

   Copy and move, and into the groove   77

   Access music files over a network   78

   Access your media from anywhere   80

New ways to play music   83

   Use a Jump List to access your music   83

   New playback modes   83

Sync an MP3 player   84

Do Burn, Rip, Visualizations, Pictures, Videos, and Playlists
still work the same way?   85

Review   88

Experiment   89

6	**Windows Media Player vs Windows Media Center**	**91**
	Get organized	92
	Watch a video	93
	Media Center	94
	Configure Media Center's Media Libraries	96
	So what's new in Media Center?	98
	Media Player or Media Center, which is better?	101
	Review	104
	Experiment	105
7	**Watch TV on your computer**	**107**
	Is your computer TV-ready?	108
	Set up a TV tuner	109
	Improve the picture	111
	Record some TV!	112
	Is it really possible to fill up your computer's hard drive in only a few weeks?	114
	Tweak the record settings	115
	What does Media Center offer sports fans?	116
	Watch Internet TV	118
	Review	120
	Experiment	121
8	**Shortcuts and personalization save time**	**123**
	Copy or move your documents	124
	Improved and categorized searches	124
	Filter the Start Search results list	125
	Taskbar improvements	127
	Pin items to the Taskbar	128
	Take advantage of Jump Lists	129
	Remove items from the Notification Area and stop alerts and notifications	130
	Reduce interruptions	132
	Automatically connect to networks	132
	Disable Snap	133
	Change user account control settings	134
	Use keyboard shortcuts	135
	Change AutoPlay Settings	136
	Review	138
	Experiment	140

Contents

9 Organize data with Libraries   **143**

How do Libraries work?   **144**

Use Libraries for data management   145

Create your own Libraries   **148**

Use Search inside a Library folder   149

Add an external drive or network share   150

Review   **152**

Experiment   **153**

10 User accounts secure your computer   **155**

Which user account is best?   **156**

Who's the Administrator?   157

What can Standard account users do?   157

Standard user account safety features   158

Create a user account for another user on your Windows 7 PC   **159**

Can two people share a PC effectively?   **161**

Two users can be logged in at the same time   161

Make Switch user the default setting on the Start menu (instead of Shut down)   162

Log off completely to save resources   162

The Guest account can serve as a temporary user account   163

Apply parental controls to manage the amount of time a standard user can have on the PC   164

Resolve sharing issues on a network   **166**

A Standard account should do the trick   166

Check the Network and Sharing settings   166

Create a Standard user account for yourself and only use the Administrator account in emergencies   **168**

Review   **171**

Experiment   **173**

11 Share data over a mixed network   **175**

Share data with everyone on the network with Public Folder Sharing   **176**

1. Turn on Public Folder Sharing   177

2. Move (or copy) data to Public folders   178

3. Access the Public folders from your personal folder   179

Create a shortcut to the Public folders for easy access   180

Create a Public Library   181

Share files and printers, fast   **182**

Share a folder, Library, or other area on your hard drive   182

Review   185

Experiment   187

12 Create a Windows 7 HomeGroup   189

What's a HomeGroup?   190

Find out if you have a HomeGroup, and, if not, create or join one   190

Create a HomeGroup   191

Join a HomeGroup   192

HomeGroup permissions   192

HomeGroup benefits and personalization   194

Keep specific files and folders from being shared   196

Share personal folders and other Libraries   197

Link on online ID with a user account   198

Network and sharing fixes   200

Review   202

Experiment   204

13 Keep your PC in shape   207

Stay safe online   208

Prevent Internet Explorer from storing data about browsing sessions   208

Internet Explorer reports a site's unsafe   209

Change the Pop-up blocker settings   209

Deal with pop-up messages that state your computer isn't secure, has a virus, or isn't performing to its potential   211

Find and resolve problems with the Action Center   211

Find and resolve problems using Windows Defender   213

Secure your computer with Windows Update   215

Maintain your computer   216

Review   219

Experiment   221

Index   223

About the author

Joli Ballew is a technical author, a technology trainer, and Web site manager in the Dallas area. She holds several certifications including MCSE, A+, MCTS, and MCDST. In addition to writing, she teaches computer classes at the local junior college, and works as a network administrator and Web designer for two Dallas-based companies.

She's written over three dozen books in 10 years, including *Degunking Windows* (awarded the IPPY award for best computer book of the year in 2005), *CNet Do-It-Yourself 24 Mac Projects*, *PC Magazine Office 2007 Solutions*, and several "*In Simple Steps*" books for Pearson Education in the United Kingdom.

In her free time, she enjoys yard work, exploring the newest gadgets, exercising at the local gym, and teaching her cats, Pico and Lucy, tricks. Before becoming a writer, Joli was a Texas public-school teacher for 10 years, teaching classes ranging from 7th grade General Math to high-school Algebra and Geometry.

Acknowledgments

It's great to be writing for John Wiley & Sons again, and I'd like to thank Chris Webb for entrusting me with this new series of books. I believe **No Problem!** will be a huge success. I'd like to thank Louise Barr too, for being so meticulous and for all of her efforts. I think she spent more time editing this book than I spent writing it. There are additional team members that deserve acknowledgment including Juliet Booker, Ellie Scott, Louise Breinholt, and Chloe Tunnicliffe, and I am thankful to have been able to work with them all.

I am thankful for many other things too, and I am fully aware of all of the blessings in my life. My 89-year-old father successfully lives alone even after my mom's passing a little over a year ago. He still drives, shops, and makes his own decisions, making my life much easier than it could be were the situation any different. I myself have been blessed with the best adoptive parents a person could want, good health, a strong, smart, loving, and capable daughter, and a great doctor. I have a wonderful family, including Jennifer, Andrew, Dad, and Cosmo. I'm amazed they are able to put up with my moods, my ups, my neutrals, and my downs. We look out for each other and manage life day by day. We may be small but we're strong!

I am also thankful for my agent, Neil Salkind from Studio B and the Salkind Literary Agency. He always looks out for me, provides new opportunities, and forces me to think out of the box when it comes to new projects. There's always a new technology or gadget, a new publisher, or a new book series to discover. Neil has my back, and offers unconditional support. Even when I'm wrong, I'm right, at least in his eyes. I doubt many people have someone like that in their lives.

And finally, I'd like say to all of you that are in a rush, it's okay to slow down a little. It's fine to stop and smell the flowers; it's heartwarming to donate some time to help others; it's okay to take time for yourself, whether it's to start a new hobby, spend time alone, meditate, pray, visit friends, or do any other thing that brings you peace and happiness. So relax, sit back, enjoy the book, and make time for yourself!

How to use this book

You want to learn new skills. You want to learn them fast. And you want to remember more, too. You don't have time to wade through any more books over and over because the information didn't stick.

⇨ Can you learn things fast and still remember them?

⇨ People forget stuff. *Lots* of stuff. Can a book help you learn better and remember more?

No Problem!

No Problem! books are aimed at anyone who needs to get up and running fast. No Problem! takes advantage of your natural learning rhythms to help you:

⇨ Learn faster and solve your problems sooner.

⇨ Avoid forgetting and remember new information better and for longer.

⇨ Follow a variety of paths through that suit your style of learning.

Your brain's already wired for this type of learning, so there's no complicated system you need to understand or any one-size-fits-all method. Choose the features within each book that feel most natural for you, making your learning experience as unique as you are.

No Problem! books have **multiple learning paths** so you can choose how you learn. Select the path that works for you, or use all of them, No Problem!

→ In a rush? No Problem! For a *quick path*, look out for the highlighted text to learn just what you need to know to get moving.

→ Prefer to *take notes* while you learn? No Problem! We've already sprinkled loads of notes and quick tips throughout the book, and left you plenty of room to take your own.

→ Like to learn by doing? No Problem! The Play with it and Experiment features give you the hands-on guidance you need.

→ Need a detailed step-by-step guide? No Problem! Combine *all* the learning paths for a comprehensive workshop.

How do each of these features work and how will they help you learn your way and remember more?

This book is like a recipe

Have you ever followed a recipe for baking a cake? Did you have to learn about ingredients, cooking temperatures and the history of baking before you baked your cake? No! You just got the ingredients together, followed the recipe and used what you already knew about cooking other things to help you bake a delicious cake.

The chapters in No Problem! books are like recipes. They skip all the historical detail and the stuff you don't need so you learn just the stuff you *do* need to help you bake some delicious new knowledge right into your brain.

Start right at the beginning and you've got a lot of dull, uninteresting stuff to get through before you can start on what's really interesting.

Start by building on pre-existing knowledge and you don't have to waste a bunch of time setting up the context. You get to focus on the interesting stuff sooner.

Active learning helps you remember

Simply reading about something is passive and passive learning doesn't stick in your brain for the long term. So how can you improve your odds of remembering what you're about to learn?

Remembering is experiential. You remember:

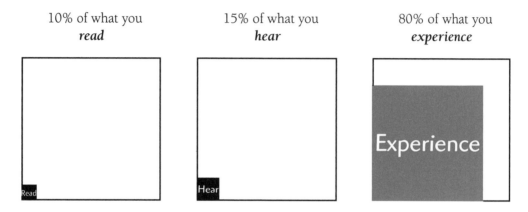

| 10% of what you *read* | 15% of what you *hear* | 80% of what you *experience* |

Did you ever see a swimming class shivering pool-side while the instructor drew diagrams on a whiteboard? No! You learn to swim by *swimming*. So it makes sense to learn this topic by **DOING**.

So the trick is to *experience* what you're here to learn. How can we help with that?

Your brain learns best when the new information it's taking in is personal, when you're experiencing it first-hand. So this book is written to keep you active. We added elements that encourage you to take what you just learned and Play with it or even to Experiment more deeply with your new knowledge to test it and strengthen it.

This is technically known as **Experiential Learning** and it's fun! Seriously, working along with the examples in the chapter will help you understand the basic concepts, but playing with them to stretch yourself and testing out new ideas is a great way to build on that knowledge.

Best of all, because you're learning your way, you're making stronger links to the new material and your personal experiences of learning—what works, what needs tweaking, what didn't work, but you fixed—will help lodge that knowledge in your brain for the longer term.

Link new knowledge to what you already know

Throughout the chapters, we suggest places for you to 'Make a link'. This is the key information you need to learn and the best way to do that is to link it to something you already know.

Sometimes a link is suggested, but if you can think of a better, more vivid or personal link, no problem. Your own links are *way* more memorable than anything we could ask you to remember. But how do you make good, strong links?

Make stronger links

Did you know you can turn the letters of the word rhythm into a short phrase to help you remember how to spell it? "**R**hythm **H**as **Y**our **T**wo **H**ips **M**oving." The first letter of each word spells out the word "rhythm".

This link is super-sticky because it shortens the words into an acronym that is the word you want to remember. This phrase is double memorable because it uses several of your senses. You can picture yourself (visual) dancing (kinetic) and moving your two hips in a nightclub (smell) to the **rhythm** of a funky tune (aural) in the background.

Senses help make information more memorable because the new abstract knowledge is stored along with the physical information from your senses. That helps your brain not only memorize the information, but recall it later because it gives your brain more paths back to the knowledge via the acronym, or the picture of the nightclub with all the associated information from your senses.

Make a link

Ask yourself, how can I learn this? What memory aids can I use?

▶ Is there a common acronym or rhyme to get it to stick, or can I make up my own and make it really vivid?

▶ Can I picture myself using this new knowledge to achieve something?

▶ Is this new knowledge *like* something that I already know about?

> **Note: Write while you're reading.**
>
> Writing (rather than typing) information helps build better links when your brain stores information. Plus, being able to revisit the "Aha!" moments that you had while you were working through the chapter when you review it triggers all kinds of related feelings and memories to help you store and recall the information better.
>
> Make a list/keep a diary/write in a notebook to record your progress and discoveries as you work through this book. Later, you can refer back to your notes as part of your Review.

Mysteries are memorable

The **Intro** and **No Problem!** in each chapter orients you with a kind of big, red YOU ARE HERE and then shows you the route you'll take to get to your goal for the chapter, but only at a very high level.

Giving the solution or goal doesn't give any information about how to make the journey—whether there are alligators in the swamp, snakes in the jungle, or pirates on the high sea—but it gives you a bare bones idea of where you're going.

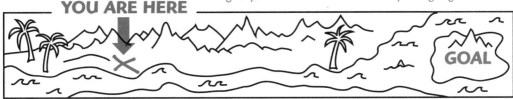

What was the first thing you did when you looked at the map? Did you try to work out how to get from "Here" to the "Goal"? Surely giving the solution at the start is counterintuitive, so how does this feature work?

Your brain loves a mystery. Ever get sucked in to watching a game featuring teams you don't support? Once you'd started watching your brain wanted to know who won. Your brain looks at problems from every angle, running them against what it already knows and predicting what will happen, then it experiments, notes what happens and tries again after making any necessary adjustments.

You've been experimenting since you started the chapter!

Why 'take a break' before the end of each chapter?

While you're learning, your concentration looks like the mouth in a smiley face. It starts high, dips in the middle, then rises again towards the end of the learning period. So you'll remember more from the start and end of the session.

Spend too long learning without a break and you'll remember less and less from the middle and end of the session . . . The right-hand side of the smile drops lower than the left.

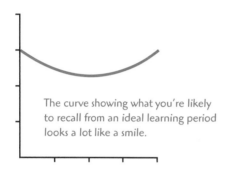

The curve showing what you're likely to recall from an ideal learning period looks a lot like a smile.

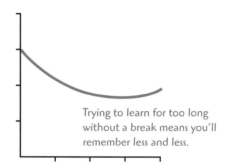

Trying to learn for too long without a break means you'll remember less and less.

So how long is just right?

The best learning periods are 20–50 minutes long. So the trick is to break your learning sessions into 20–50 minute blocks with 5–10 minute breaks in between

It sounds completely counterintuitive, huh? But, just like dreaming is your brain's way of sorting through the day's experiences while you sleep, taking a break during learning helps your brain make better links. Your brain likes to sift through all the new material and store it away. It stores stuff away best until around 10 minutes *after* you stopped learning.

So how do you work out where to take a break?

> **Tip:** We can't know how long it will take you to work through a chapter, but the chapters are structured to allow for natural breaks, so it should be pretty easy to take regular breaks every 20–50 minutes.
>
> At the very least we think your brain will thank you if you take a 10-minute break when you finish the chapter and before you come back to do the Review and Experiment, so we've put a reminder in every chapter to take a break there.
>
> **Yes. We're seriously encouraging you to close this book and go do something unrelated for a few minutes!**

Learn. Review. Repeat.

A massive 80% of what you learn is lost after 1–2 days. Despite all your best efforts, your brain still wants to toss out most of what you want it to learn. Ack. All is lost. . .

But wait! Apart from the stuff your body does automatically to keep you alive (breathing, heart beating, etc) you *had to learn everything else you do*. Eating, reading, dating, diving with sharks. How did you learn to do these things if your brain is so determined to forget so much of what you want it to learn?

Your brain needs to repeat new information to save it to long-term memory for good. How will you repeat what you've learned to help burn it into your memory?

Take some time at the end of each day to review your notes from that day's learning. That helps your brain realize this is stuff it needs to keep around. We added Reviews to every chapter to help you along.

Do another review in a week's time, then another after a month and another after six months and so on and your knowledge and recall will quickly become rock solid.

Tip: Reviewing isn't a big deal. Take a few minutes at the end of every chapter to make notes on what you remember, then compare them with the notes you made at the time. Write any information you missed in the Review and any new notes (your brain will have thought of new things in the meantime—it's constantly learning and making new links) in the margin of your original notes.

Review

In this document, you learned how to help your brain remember better.

- ↺ No Problem books are like .... , building on what you already know to help you build delicious new things.
- ↺ .... learning helps you learn up to ....% more than reading alone.
- ↺ Make .... from what you already .... to new knowledge you want to ....
- ↺ Mysteries are ....
- ↺ Taking a break helps your brain ....

And you did it all by understanding how the brain works to help your brain learn faster, naturally.

1 Be more efficient with Windows 7

You just got a new computer with Windows 7; you're excited because there are new ways to move around the Desktop, navigate through open windows, and even a way to make all the windows (except the one you want to work with) disappear with a swipe of the mouse. But when you start up your machine, it doesn't look very familliar:

⇨ The Taskbar looks kind of transparent and it's got a bunch of different icons on it.

⇨ The Start menu's changed.

⇨ Even the Desktop background is new.

You want to dive in and play with the cool new features, but because everything looks so different, where do you start?

No Problem!

Learning how to use Windows 7 is like learning anything else; start with the simple stuff and work your way up. Although it *looks* different, this is still Windows and many things work exactly the way you expect them to. Most likely you'll have spent time futzing with *how your computer looks* in the past and believe it or not:

⇨ Choosing a screen saver

⇨ Setting a Desktop background

⇨ Messing with Desktop shortcuts

are great ways to learn how to move around in Windows 7. So let's start with something you're already comfortable with, but fasten your seat belts because along the way you'll learn about the surprising new ways to manipulate your Desktop.

Make Windows 7 look more familiar

The Desktop looks different and things aren't in the same place as before, so where do you begin? Let's start with something you already know how to do. Take a look at the Desktop and think about what you'd like to change.

- ☐ Do you want a different Desktop background image?
- ☐ Do you want quick access to your personal file folder?
- ☐ Do you want the picture on the Desktop to change occasionally?

Of course you do, and in Windows 7 the sky's the limit. But how will you change any of that stuff since *everything* looks so different now?

Make a link

Some things may be organized a little differently than you're used to, but **many tools and features work the same way they always have**.

Go ahead and right-click the Desktop and choose **Personalize** from the pop-up menu. This works just the same way it did in previous versions of Windows.

Play with it

Take a look at your options. Spend a little time familiarizing yourself with the Personalize window and make sure to get the Desktop just how you like it. Here are some things you might want to try:

→ Change the picture on the Desktop.

→ Adjust the screen resolution.

→ Select a screen saver.

How are these personalization options different or similar to what you're used to? For instance, is it easier or harder to change the mouse pointer or your account picture?

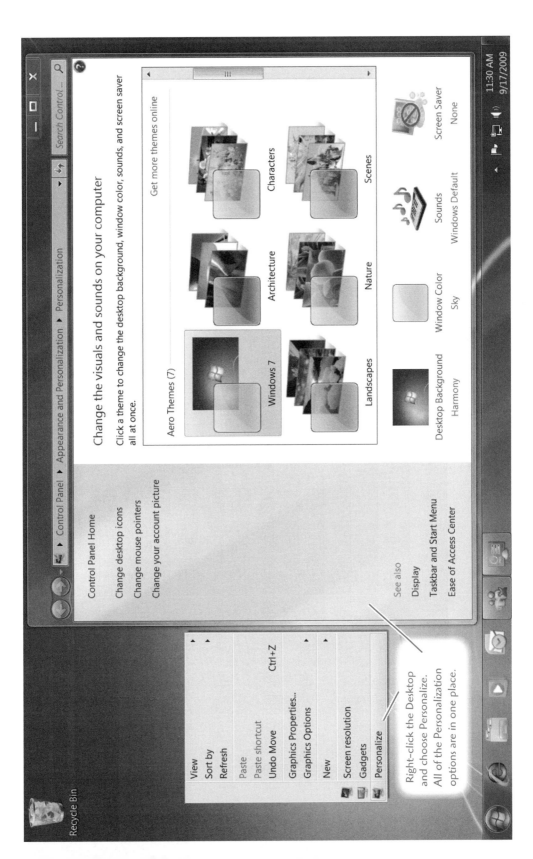

Work faster with Windows 7's new features

Windows 7 lets you configure the Desktop to make your workflow more efficient, but how will you streamline things if you don't know how they work?

Right now you have to work through the Start menu or All Programs to find what you want, or you have to type a keyword in the Start Search window, but Windows 7 lets you put icons for things you use every day right on the Desktop, so you can access them with a single click.

Go ahead and create **shortcuts** on the Desktop for your favorite programs. How did you do this before? Find the program in the All Programs menu, right-click it, and choose **Send to**, then **Desktop (create shortcut)**. It's the same in Windows 7 as it's been since Windows 98.

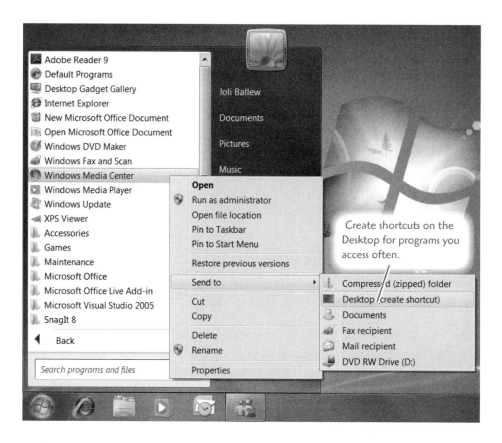

Do you like to have **icons on your Desktop** for things like Documents, Pictures, Music, Computer, etc? Add these from **Change Desktop Items** in the Personalization window, or from the Start menu with the familiar right-click to access **Show on Desktop**.

Use both methods for populating your Desktop with your favorite icons until you have it looking the way you want. Do you prefer one method for adding icons over the other? Why?

How's your Desktop looking now? Are you happy with this size and position of your new icons? You can reposition icons on your Desktop and even change their size. How do you think you'd do that?

As with other "change how the computer looks" tasks, right-click the Desktop to get started. Click **View** in the pop-up menu to change the size of your icons and sort them in a specific way. Try Large icons. If you like, it, leave it. If not, try Small icons or Medium icons until you're happy with your arrangement.

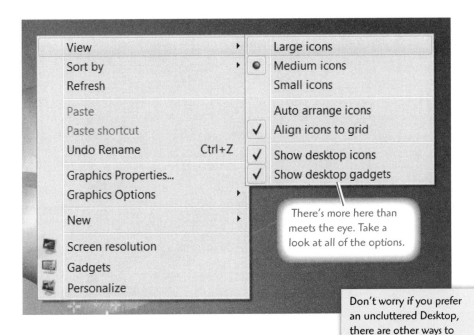

Take a look at the other things you can change about how your Desktop's arranged and think about how you might use them to help you work more efficiently. Do you like that your icons are aligned in an imaginary grid or would you rather them be positioned exactly where you want them?

Don't worry if you prefer an uncluttered Desktop, there are other ways to get to the things you use every day faster than clicking through a bunch of menus, including using the new Start Search feature, detailed in chapter 8.

If you want to arrange the items alphabetically, you can do that too, from the **Sort by** menu. Oh, and when you're done, click and drag your Desktop icons around a bit. You may find moving them to different areas of the screen helps you find and use them more easily.

Access information quickly with gadgets

Ever been in the middle of writing a report and wished you could get up-to-date currency exchange rates without having to switch focus completely to a web browser? How about accessing reports on the weather, what's on TV, or even performing a web search? And how do you keep track of ever-changing data like upcoming appointments in Outlook, updates to your eBay bids, or even how much battery life you have left on your laptop? Imagine how much time you'd save if you could do all these things, and more, right from your Desktop. Luckily, it's all possible with **gadgets**.

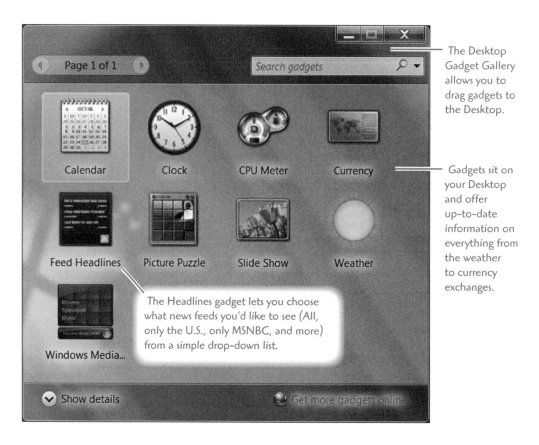

The Desktop Gadget Gallery allows you to drag gadgets to the Desktop.

Gadgets sit on your Desktop and offer up-to-date information on everything from the weather to currency exchanges.

The Headlines gadget lets you choose what news feeds you'd like to see (All, only the U.S., only MSNBC, and more) from a simple drop-down list.

If you're coming from Windows XP, gadgets will be a surprising, (but welcome) new feature. Think of **gadgets** as little mini-programs you can configure with your own local data. If you're coming from Vista, well, there's no longer a "sidebar" that holds the gadgets (which was limiting); now you simply add gadgets and place them wherever you want on the Desktop.

Play with it

Where do you think you'd find the gadgets? Right, go to the All Programs list, then **Desktop Gadget Gallery**. Once the Gallery's open, simply **drag the gadgets you want to the Desktop**.

Click the wrench icon to configure a gadget.

Once the gadget is on the Desktop, hover your mouse over any gadget to access the options to personalize it.

Search for your location in the Weather gadget's personalization options. Type the city and state, and click the magnifying glass.

Manage multiple windows with Shake, Snap, and Peek

Have you ever had a bunch of windows from different programs open all at once and needed to find something specific in just one of them? How about if you have a few windows open and you want to focus on one and minimize all the others? What if you needed to look at something saved to your Desktop? How much time could you save if windows were easier to work with?

Shake, **Snap**, and **Peek** are three new ways to work with multiple windows. Think about what each of these words means and how you apply these actions in your everyday life for a moment. Shaking, snapping, and peeking can be quite handy. On a computer, these actions can make you more efficient as you move through open windows and work across multiple windows. What do you think each of these Desktop enhancements will offer?

→ Why do you shake something, and what happens when you do?
What do you think will happen when you use Shake with a window?

....

→ What can you think of that snaps into place? Why is that useful?
How do you think Snap will affect a window?

....

→ You peek at something if you only need a quick ....
What do you think Peek will let you do if you have a bunch of open windows?

....

Let's see if you were right, starting with Shake.

Shake

When you have several windows open at the same time because you're multi-tasking and you need to switch focus to just one of the open windows, selecting all the other open windows and minimizing them individually takes an age and breaks your train of thought. Sounds like you need to **Shake** out those windows.

What happens when you *shake* something? The contents fall out of or off whatever it is you're shaking, like salt coming out of a salt shaker or dust coming off a rug. What do you think would happen if you had several open windows on your Desktop and you grabbed the top of one and shook it?

1. Open several windows from the Start menu. You could open Documents, Help and Support, Computer, Music, and Devices and Printers to try this.

2. Choose one window, perhaps Computer, click once with the mouse on its title bar, and shake it left and right.

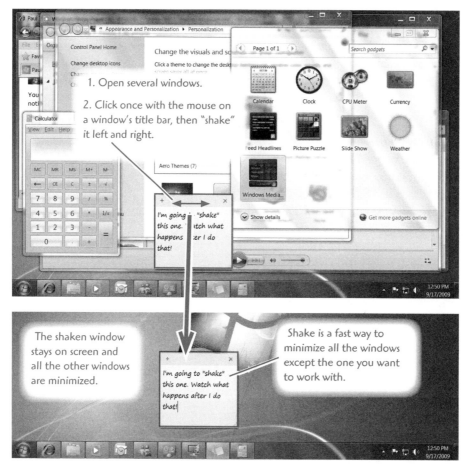

Don't just read these instructions, *try it out for yourself*. When you have many windows open and you're finding it hard to see the forest for the trees, Shake minimizes all the other open windows and leaves only the "shaken" window on the screen.

How do you think you'd get all your windows back? Shake the lone window again and watch all of the minimized windows reappear.

Now you know all about Shake, what do you think will happen when you try the Snap feature?

Snap

How many times have you tried to position a window so it takes up half the screen? Maybe you wanted to compare two versions of a document or check some data. That's two windows to position and it's pretty fiddly, huh? How much time would it save if your windows could **Snap** into a special position? Windows 7 gives you just such a feature:

1. Open your personal folder on the Start menu. It's the icon with your name on it and has a related picture.

2. Click and drag the title bar of that window to the **top right corner** of the screen. What happens to the window?

3. Now, open the Computer window (also from the Start menu), but drag the title bar of this new window to the **top left** of the screen. What happens this time?

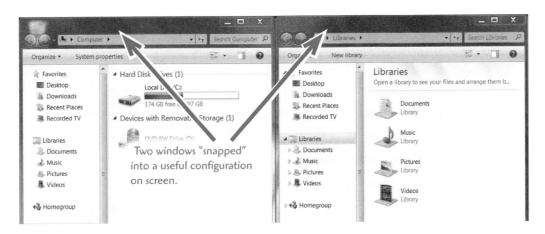

Two windows "snapped" into a useful configuration on screen.

When would this particular window arrangement be useful? How often have you used this kind of window arrangement? Next time you find yourself needing *two windows side-by-side* like this, give **Snap** a shot.

Play with it

Drag a couple more windows to the top left and right corners of the screen to Snap them into place. Make sure you can easily arrange two windows so they're side-by-side like the Libraries and Computer windows before.

Now see what happens when you drag a window to the top center of the screen. Any window will do. Grab it and drag it upwards, to the center of the screen. What happens?

Okay, let's try something else. What happens when you grab the title bar of a maximized window and drag downward?

When would being able to maximize and restore a window quickly be useful?

Peek

Have you ever had a ton of windows open and needed to see something on the Desktop? Ugh, how much of a pain is it to minimize everything to get there? Minimizing everything can be a drastic step if you have multiple windows open, especially if you aren't familiar with Shake. If you're coming from XP or Vista you know the problem all too well. Click the Show Desktop icon to see the Weather gadget, and then use the Taskbar to restore *all* of the minimized windows back to the Desktop. More pain. There has to be an easier way . . .

Peek is a new feature on the Taskbar that allows you to see what's on the Desktop without minimizing everything. And even better, you only have to hover your mouse over the proper area of the Taskbar; you don't even have to click the mouse. The Peek spot is just to the right of the Notification area. It's a small, transparent, rectangle.

If you use gadgets, this is a handy way to check the weather, stock prices, or currency exchanges without leaving the program you're working in.

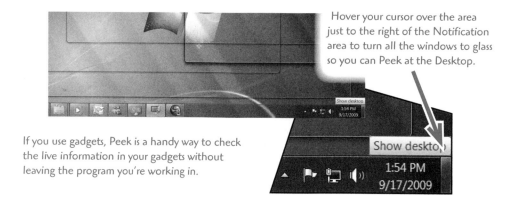

Hover your cursor over the area just to the right of the Notification area to turn all the windows to glass so you can Peek at the Desktop.

If you use gadgets, Peek is a handy way to check the live information in your gadgets without leaving the program you're working in.

Make a link

Your brain remembers things that are personal to you way better than things that we could tell you to remember. If you were a little hazy on one of Shake, Snap or Peek's superpowers and how it worked, take some time to make the picture of them in your head more vivid. What color costumes are they wearing? Is Peek invisible, too? How would each of them talk?

Your brain loves things that are funny, scary, surprising, smelly (it's true; you could imagine the smell of the vanilla or chocolate coating on your Desktop heroes), you can even imagine what movement you make to invoke a superpower. Try that now; use your hands to play Shake, Snap and Peek charades and mime the different moves you make with the mouse to call each superhero.

You might feel a little silly miming or attaching smells to concepts, but your brain will thank you for taking the time to make strong links from your own knowledge to the new information you want it to learn.

Practice often to improve your recall

It's also a good idea to go over the review questions again in a day's time, then try the questions again in:

→ A week's time

→ A month's time

→ Six months' time

→ A year's time, and so on.

If you find anything's missing or harder to remember, take some time to work on just those bits and make stronger links.

Take a break

Take a break and walk around. Grab a drink, read a magazine article, or even go for a short walk. Give your brain about 10 minutes' break then come back here for the Review and the Experiment. It doesn't matter what you do, and it sounds counterintuitive, but try not to actively think about what you just learned and your brain will take care of the rest!

Review

It's time to do a quick review of all the ways you can personalize your computer, and how you can incorporate the new Desktop enhancement features into your everyday computer tasks.

Fill in the spaces below to review your knowledge of each topic.

- ↻ To change your Desktop background right-click the .... Did this work the same way you expected it to?

- ↻ The Personalization window also includes options to change the .... scheme or .... color as well as a bunch of new .... and backgrounds.

- ↻ To create a shortcut to a program, find the program in All .... , right-click it and choose Send To: .... (Create ....).

- ↻ The .... menu also lets you change the .... of the icons on your Desktop.

- ↻ Gadgets are like mini-programs you can add your .... data to.

- ↻ Access the full list of gadgets via the .... that can be found in All Programs.

- ↻ .... an open window and all the other windows are minimized.

- ↻ Drag the title bar of a window to the top-left of your screen to .... What does Snap do to a window if you drag its title bar to the top center of the screen? ....

- ↻ When you've got a bunch of windows open and you want to .... at the Desktop without minimizing all the windows, you hover your cursor over which area?

  ....

How did you do?

It's not a problem if anything's a little hazy; just go back and re-read the content in the chapter and take some extra time to think of ways to remember the new information.

> When you're done with your Review, the very best way to make sure this new information sticks is to practice using these new skills as you go through the next few chapters.

Experiment

The best way to really cement these features and techniques into your long-term memory is to expand on the techniques you learned in the chapter by using them and taking them just one step further.

Here are some suggestions for your experiment using techniques covered in this chapter.

Change the sound scheme

You're probably pretty familiar with the sounds your computer makes. There's the "critical stop" sound (a low sound - dah, dump), the "exit Windows" sound (a high sound - plink!), and the "empty Recycle Bin" sound (the sound of paper crumpling). You may not know it, but that's a sound scheme, specifically, the Windows default sound scheme.

You can select a different sound scheme from the Personalization options. Try Festival, Delta, Quirky, or Sonata, or any of the 14 options. Just open the Personalization window and click Sounds to get started.

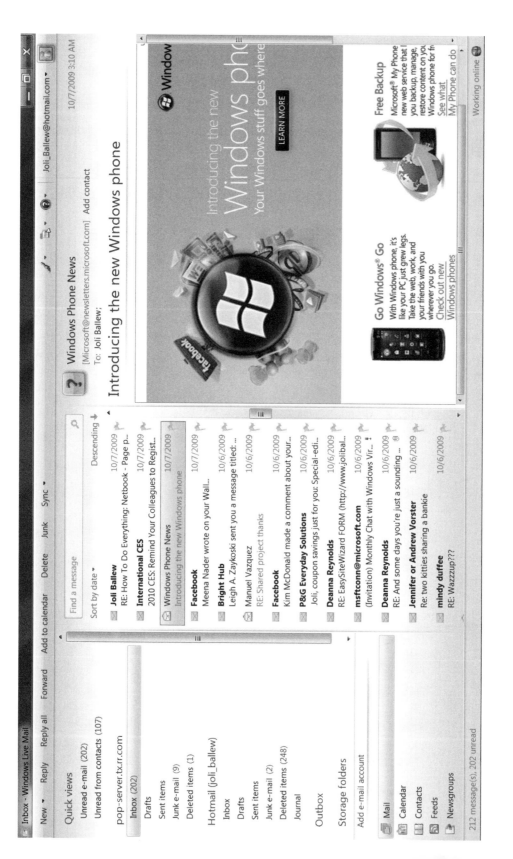

2 Where's the e-mail program?

Windows XP has Outlook Express. Windows Vista has Mail. Windows 7 has, um, what exactly? Have you found anything even close to an e-mail program? So uh, where's the e-mail program? And . . .

⇨ If there's no e-mail program, will you have to use your Internet Service Provider's (ISP's) web mail interface?

⇨ Will you have to purchase Microsoft Outlook?

⇨ Will you have to learn a new program?

⇨ What about all your contacts and messages? If you get a new program, can they be imported or will you have to start over?

All you need is to access your e-mail, how are you going to get past all these problems?

No Problem!

You don't have to start over, and you don't have to purchase any programs to get your e-mail. Microsoft provides an e-mail client for you, online and at no cost, called Windows Live Mail, and it's bundled with other programs you can opt to include, like Windows Live Photo Gallery, Windows Live Toolbar, and Windows Live Messenger, to name a few.

Windows Live Mail looks and acts a lot like Vista's Mail and a bit like Outlook Express, so it'll be an easy transition. It was created by Microsoft, so it's definitely compatible with Windows 7. And because it's compatible with other "Live" applications, you can integrate your e-mail with your photos, Windows Live contacts, and even Internet Explorer. If you want to get up and running with e-mail as quickly as possible, and you want to be fully integrated, this is the way to go.

Windows Live Mail has to be downloaded? But I'm not online yet!

If you want to download Windows Live Mail, you need to get online first. Connecting to the Internet is easier than ever with Windows 7, so let's take a quick detour here to get online now. (If you're already online, feel free to skip ahead to page 21.)

You can connect your Windows 7 PC to the Internet the same way you currently connect, with dial-up, broadband, satellite, or another option. If you have a cable modem and a router, connecting is as simple as plugging the new computer into an available Ethernet port in the router. If you have a wireless network, you'll simply turn on your new PC within range of it. These are the two most common connectivity options, and the ones we'll cover.

Connect with Ethernet

If you have a home network and a router, stop what you're doing and find a spare Ethernet cable. Use that cable to connect your new PC to the router. If you have a cable modem and no router, unplug the computer currently connected to the modem and plug in your new Windows 7 PC. Go ahead and do that now, and then come back here. Write down any notes about this in the margin.

What happens when Windows 7 "sees" that it is connected to a network or a cable modem? You're prompted to choose a **network type**. There are three:

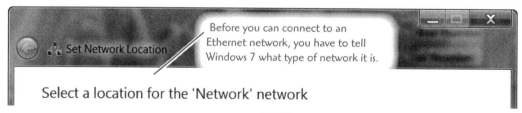

Before you can connect to an Ethernet network, you have to tell Windows 7 what type of network it is.

Select a location for the 'Network' network

 Home network

→ **Home**: This is the type of network you have in your home. It's secure and private, and you manage it.

 Work network

→ **Work**: This is the type of network you have at work. It's secure and is managed by an IT person or IT staff.

 Public network

→ **Public**: This is the type of network you connect to when you take your laptop to the local public library, hotel, or pub. Often, access is free, and unsecured.

This is the only thing that's changed in Windows 7, at least as far as making the connection goes; you have to state what kind of network you're connecting to before Windows will allow you to connect. So, decide what kind of network you're joining and click your selection in the list.

There are just a few caveats:

You may be prompted to turn on Network Discovery. This allows computers on the network to see your PC and allows your PC to see network resources (like computers, files, and printers). *If you see the prompt and you're connecting to a network you trust, opt to enable* **Network Discovery**.

Once you're connected, click the Network icon in the Taskbar, and click Open Network and Sharing Center. From here you can manage your network and connections.

The Network and Sharing Center shows your working connection to the Internet, among other things.

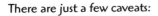

This is the Network icon you'll need to click on to access the Network and Sharing Center.

Connect to a wireless network

If you have a wireless network, you're already familiar with how to connect to it. Simply *make sure you're within range of the network access point* and when prompted, click **Connect**. As with Ethernet networks, there are three network types: Home, Work, and Public.

What if you didn't get a prompt?

1. Click the **wireless network** icon on the Taskbar. This is a new icon, and is where you'll access everything network-related.

2. Click the network you want to connect to in the dialog that pops up.

3. When you've selected a network, click the Connect button that appears.

4. If you've secured your network, you'll be prompted to type the security key.

As with an Ethernet network, you may be prompted to turn on **Network Discovery**. This allows computers on the network to see your PC and for your PC to see network resources (like computers, files, and printers). If you see the prompt *and you're connecting to a network you trust*, opt to **enable Network Discovery**. Otherwise, it'll automatically be configured.

5. Once you're connected, click the **Network** icon in the Taskbar. What does it show you now?

Play with it

See if you can connect to a free, wireless hotspot. Take your wireless-enabled Windows 7 laptop or netbook to your local coffee house, library, or hotel. Make sure to pick a place that offers a free Wi-Fi hotspot.

Watch for a pop-up that says wireless networks are available, and if you don't see one, click the Network icon in the Taskbar. Locate the free hotspot in the list, click it, and connect.

If you don't know where the closest hotspot is, visit **www.openwifispots.com** and type in your city, state, and zip code, or choose a major city from the list before you go. Write the locations you find here, and then take a drive to see how your laptop or netbook fares!

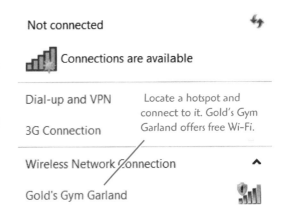

Make notes for the next time you connect

Connecting to a network is not something you do every day. But it *is* something you'll do each time a guest comes with a laptop, or you bring a new netbook or hand-held PC into the house. Take a moment to answer the questions below so you can refer to them later.

1. Where can you locate the Network icon?

   ....

2. What can you access by clicking the Network icon?

   ....

3. What kind of network did you connect to: Ethernet or wireless?

   ....

4. Did you choose Home, Work, or Public after making the connection? Why?

   ....

5. Did you enable Network Discovery? Why or why not?

   ....

6. Did you have any problems creating the connection? If you did, how did you resolve them?

   ....

7. Looking at the Network and Sharing Center, what can you do there?

   ....

If you get stuck on any of these, look back over those pages.

Download and install Windows Live Mail

Great! You're connected to the Internet. Now, how do you get Windows Live Mail? That's the easy part; it's just a simple download. Go to `http://download.live.com` and work through the download process. That means you'll need to choose the Windows Live Essentials programs you want.

We recommend you get **Mail**, **Photo Gallery**, and the **Toolbar**, and if you plan to do any instant messaging, get **Messenger** too. There are others, which you can see here. Check the ones you want, start the download and complete the installation.

> You'll meet many of these Live applications later in the book. Don't worry if you didn't download them now; you can always grab them when we get to them.

Windows Live

Install the programs you think you'll use. We recommend Mail, Photo Gallery, and Toolbar at least.

Choose the programs you want to install

Click each program name for details.

- ☑ 👥 Messenger
- ☑ 🗐 Mail
- ☑ 🖼 Photo Gallery
- ☑ 🔧 Toolbar
- ☑ ✒ Writer
- ☑ 👪 Family Safety

You already have these programs:

- ✅ 📧 Microsoft Office Outlook...
- ✅ 🔲 Microsoft Office Live Ad...

Messenger

Send instant messages to contacts or groups, play games, share pictures as you chat, and see what's new with people you know.

Installed with this program:

- Microsoft Application Error Reporting
- Microsoft Visual Studio Runtime
- Windows Live Communications Platform
- Segoe UI Font
- Windows Live Call

Space needed:	166 MB
Space available:	128 GB

[Install]   [Cancel]

Note: It's unlikely that Windows Live Essentials came preinstalled on your new PC. However, if it was, you'll be informed the programs are already installed during the download process, or you can look for them yourself by clicking Start, then All Programs, and looking for Windows Live.

Why sign up for a Windows Live ID?

When the download completes, you'll be prompted to obtain a Windows Live ID. This is an optional thing; you don't have to have one. But a Windows Live ID lets you more easily link all of your Live applications, and for that reason it's highly recommended. Are there any other reasons that are *even more* compelling than synchronizing all your programs?

If you have existing Windows Live contacts, perhaps those you've added with older versions of Messenger or Live Call, your Windows Live ID will automatically add those contacts to Live Mail. And because all the Windows Live programs are compatible and collaborative, you'll see those contacts in other Live programs too.

You get 25 GB of free, online storage. That means you can store your data on an Internet server to back it up, share it with others, or access it from any computer that offers Internet access, like a netbook, campus PC, or even a hotel lobby computer.

Tip: You like those perks you get from a Windows Live ID? Want more? Here's a list of some of the reasons why you should get a Windows Live ID:

When you sign in to a Live program with a Windows Live ID, you can easily access your e-mail, Live Photo Gallery photos, your personal blog, Messenger contacts, Xbox Live, and more, and work among them seamlessly using the Live Toolbar and Live websites.

You can easily incorporate all your social networking sites, like Facebook, Twitter, Photobucket, Flickr, and Wordpress, into your free Windows Live website.

You can create personalized groups to collaborate online with family, friends, and coworkers. Then you can create event pages for parties, collaborate on projects, or manage family affairs online and from anywhere.

Live Mail offers a free e-mail address that you could use for specific things, like making purchases online, logging into .NET services, joining newsgroups, and subscribing to Web communities to help you manage spam.

You may already have a Live ID. A Windows Live ID ends in .Live or .Hotmail. If you already have one, you can sign in to Windows Live and related applications when prompted. If you don't have one, go to `https://signup.live.com` to get one.

Set up Windows Live Mail

You've gotten online, downloaded Windows Live Mail, and even obtained a Windows Live ID. But before you can get your e-mail, there's one last step to complete. You have to tell Windows Live Mail about your existing e-mail account(s) so that it can grab your mail.

There are three methods for setting up e-mail in Windows Live Mail and you can mix and match to configure multiple e-mail accounts:

1. **Use your new Windows Live ID as an e-mail account.** Because it's a Windows Live ID, Windows Live Mail already knows the settings, so it's a breeze to set up and requires minimal intervention from you. Even if you don't need an additional e-mail address, you can use it for registering for websites or making online purchases to protect your default account from spam.

2. **Add your personal e-mail address from your ISP.** During set-up, you'll likely have to input the server names and specific settings as required. This requires an extra step, but it's no big deal, especially if you've done it before.

3. **Import existing e-mail account and messages** from Windows Mail, Windows Outlook Express 6, or another instance of Windows Live Mail on another PC. With this method, your messages are imported as well as your e-mail account information.

Don't fret, the process works about the same as Outlook Express, Mail, and even Microsoft Office Outlook. You work through a wizard to input your e-mail address, display name, password, plus any other information it asks you for, and you're up and running.

1. Use your new Windows Live ID as an e-mail account

If you have a Windows Live ID, you'll be up and running with e-mail in only a few minutes. Windows Live Mail also supports Hotmail, Yahoo! Plus, and Gmail, which means you can set those up just by inputting your account and password information here instead.

The steps are virtually identical to what you're used to in Mail and Outlook Express:

1. Click **Add e-mail account** in the **Mail** toolbar.

2. Type your new Windows Live ID and password.

3. Type your display name as you'd like it to appear in others' inboxes.

4. Click Next.

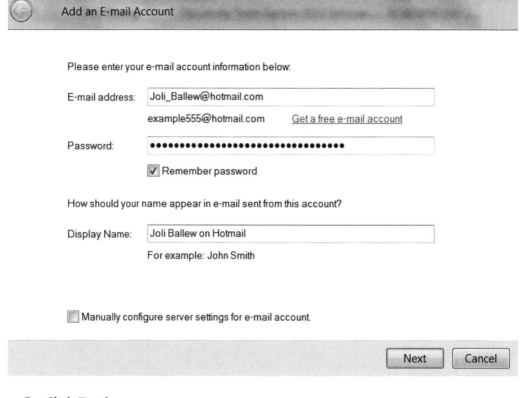

5. Click Finish.

6. Click Download to, uh, well, you know . . .

2. Add your personal e-mail address from your ISP

What if you want to use an e-mail address from Road Runner, Sprint, Verizon, or similar entity? Work through the process detailed in the previous section, but you may be asked to input information regarding the POP3 and SMTP server names. This is a common task, and you've probably done it before. You can get the required information from your ISP, their website, or from settings configured in your previous e-mail program.

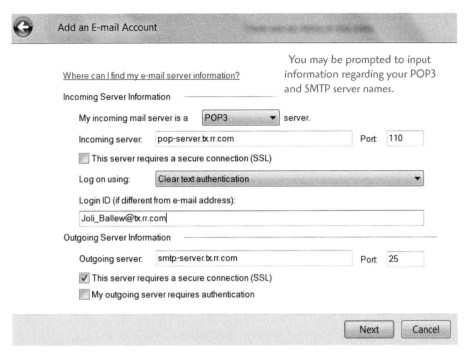

You won't always be prompted though; Windows Live Mail knows the settings for some e-mail addresses, and may fill in the information automatically. If you're prompted, locate the information and write it down here for future reference:

POP3 server name:

....

SMTP server name:

....

Authentication requirements:

....

Port requirements:

....

User name:

....

Password: Don't write it here, but do put it somewhere safe.

When you've input the required information, how will you test your account settings are working? Simple, send yourself an e-mail from that account and back to it.

3. Import an existing e-mail account and messages

You can import messages and e-mail account settings currently held in Vista's Mail, other instances of Windows Live Mail, and Windows XP's Outlook Express. This is easy if you're moving from one of these programs to Windows Live Mail on the same PC; the files are already there and Live Mail knows where to look. But what if you have a new Windows 7 PC or a newly formatted one, and your existing messages are somewhere else, most likely on another PC?

You need to figure out where your old messages are stored before you can move them into Windows Live Mail. That's because you have to work through the "import" process, and part of that process is to tell Windows Live Mail where to find the e-mails to import. The messages you're looking for will be in the previous application's **Store Folder**. But, how do you find your Store Folder and when you have, how will you copy the data in it?

Locate and copy messages to import

First you'll need to locate where your existing messages are stored on your old machine:

1. In the e-mail program on your old machine, click **Tools**, then **Options**. (If you can't see the Tools menu on the toolbar, press Alt on the keyboard.

    a. In Windows Live Mail, and Windows Mail, click the Advanced tab, then Maintenance, and Store Folder.

    b. In Outlook Express, click the Maintenance tab, then Store Folder.

2. Highlight and then copy the file location.

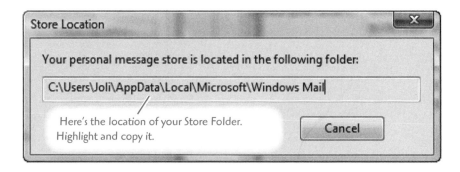

3. Close all of the windows associated with the older e-mail program.

4. On the same (older) PC, open the **Run** dialog box.

   → On Windows XP, Run is on the Start menu.

   → On Windows Vista and Windows 7, it's in All Programs>Accessories.

   → And remember, you can always search for it!

5. In the **Run** dialog box, paste the information you copied for the Store folder.

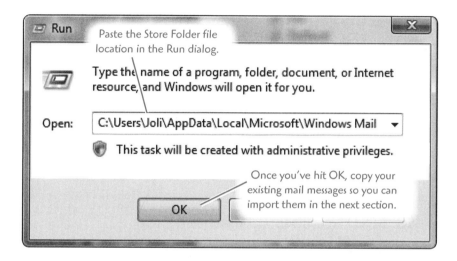

6. Click OK. The Store folder will open.

7. Select all the files and copy them.

   → Paste the files to a USB flash drive if you don't have a local area network.

   → If you do have a local network, feel free to choose any shared folder both PCs can access. Close all windows and hop back over to your Windows 7 PC.

Now that you have access to the messages you want to import, it's a simple process to import them.

Import existing messages

1. Open Windows Live Mail.

2. Press Alt to show the toolbar.

3. Click **File**>**Import**>**Messages**.

4. Select where the messages came from :

   → Microsoft Outlook Express 6

   → Windows Live Mail

   → Windows Mail

5. Click Next.

6. Click Browse to locate the messages to import on either the flash drive or shared folder. Click Next.

7. Decide whether you're going to import all your messages or just some of them.

   → To import *all messages*, click **All Folders**.

   → To import only **Selected Folders**, hold down **Ctrl** and **click** the folders to import. Click Next.

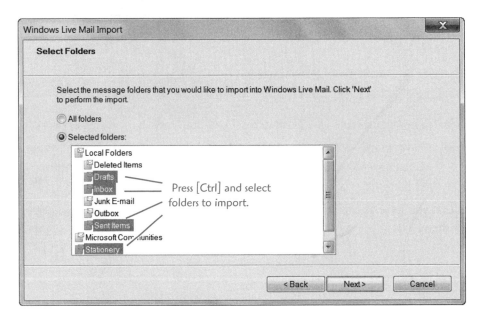

8. Wait while the import process completes.

Get your mail!

Your e-mail should come in automatically after you set up your e-mail account(s). But it's best to click **Sync** to be sure. Do you see the arrow next to the Sync button? Click it to choose just one e-mail address to sync if you have multiple addresses configured.

Tip: Do you keep a lot of e-mail in your Inbox, and want to see only the unread mail that's arrived since you last checked your mail on the old PC? Under **Quick Views**, click **Unread e-mail**. To see only unread mail from people who are your contacts, click **Unread from contacts**.

Take a break

Okay, you're all set up so reward yourself with a quick break. Stretch your legs, grab a drink, or watch the birds out the window. You'll come back refreshed and your brain will be ready to meet Live Mail.

Get to know Windows Live Mail

So you've downloaded the program, installed it and even imported your old e-mails, but how long is it going to take to get up to speed with Windows Live Mail? Have you ever used an e-mail client like Microsoft Outlook, Outlook Express, Windows Live Mail before? Great, you'll take quickly to Windows Live Mail, because Live Mail acts like every other e-mail client you've ever used.

Play with it

Windows Live Mail sure looks *familiar*. You already know more than you think you do, so jump right in and play with Windows Live Mail.

There are lots of similarities and a lot to draw on from what you already know about other e-mail clients. Here are just a few of the things you'll feel at home with.

1. The **New** button is for composing new mail. Click it to compose a new e-mail.

2. The **Reply**, **Reply all**, **Forward**, **Delete**, and **Junk buttons** are all familiar commands in the toolbar.

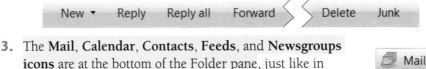

3. The **Mail**, **Calendar**, **Contacts**, **Feeds**, and **Newsgroups icons** are at the bottom of the Folder pane, just like in Microsoft Outlook. Click the icons to move among them.

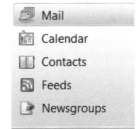

4. The arrow by the New button (see it?) lets you easily create a new photo e-mail, event, news message, contact, and ─────── folder. If you're used to Mail or Outlook Express, these are the same options as you'd find under File > New.

5. The Inbox references in the Folder pane work the same as always. Right-click the Inbox to add a new folder for organizing your e-mail.

   What other similarities do you see?

That's great and all, but what if all you want to do is configure settings like how often to check for new messages, create signatures, and configure how e-mail is composed, sent, and received?

6. Click the **Menus** button and then **Options** to access these options.

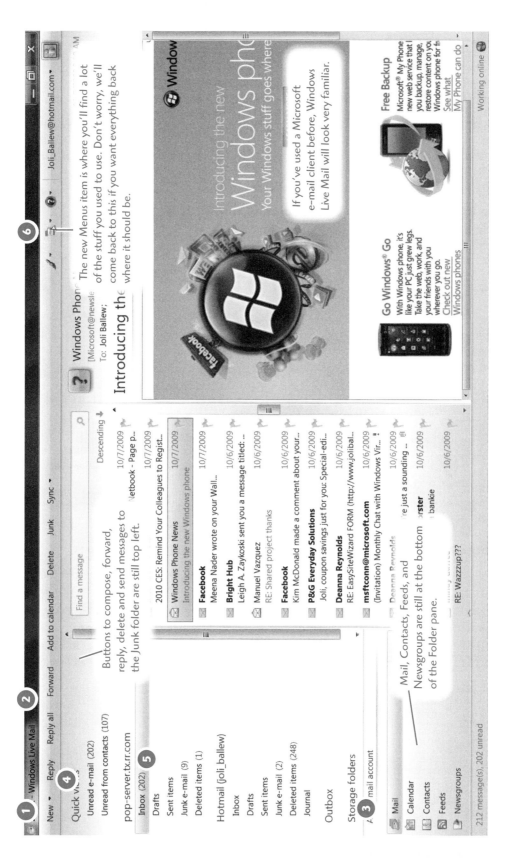

Explore the differences

So you're okay with the things that *haven't* changed. But what about the glaring differences in Windows Live Mail when you compare it to Outlook Express or Vista's Windows Mail? There are a few things that can throw you off quickly, or at least slow you down. Here's a breakdown of what to watch for.

The biggest difference: Sync replaces Send/Receive

The Send/Receive button has been replaced by the **Sync** Button. At first it seems like that's not such a big deal, but when you find yourself looking for the Send/Receive button in the days and weeks to come, you'll be pleased you took a little time now to learn that.

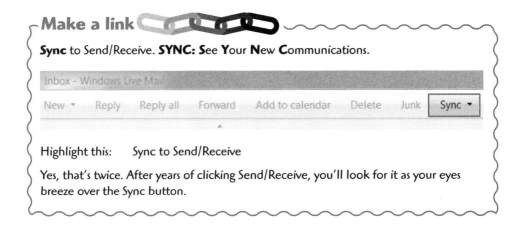

Make a link

Sync to Send/Receive. **SYNC: S**ee **Y**our **N**ew **C**ommunications.

Inbox - Windows Live Mail

New ▾   Reply   Reply all   Forward   Add to calendar   Delete   Junk   Sync ▾

Highlight this: Sync to Send/Receive

Yes, that's twice. After years of clicking Send/Receive, you'll look for it as your eyes breeze over the Sync button.

Bring back familiar items

What if you want to use the File, Edit, View, and Favorites options that the old toolbar contained? What if you liked reading your e-mail just fine when it ran across the bottom? The reading pane is on the right now; if you're used to Outlook Express can you put it back where it belongs, underneath the message list? And what about the new icons on the "Command" bar, what do they do? You don't have time to learn the nuances of Windows Live Mail; you need to know where the old stuff is and how to get to it. Today. Now.

Luckily, just because Microsoft thinks these changes are an improvement doesn't mean you have to. So is the e-mail toolbar *gone*? No, but it doesn't show by default. If you're a fan of menus, you'll want to either enable the toolbar permanently or know the trick for showing it temporarily.

→ Press the **Alt** key on the keyboard. What happens?

→ Do you want the toolbar you're familiar with—the one with File, Edit, View, Go, Tools, Actions, and Help—to show all the time? If you do, click the new **Menus** icon, and click **Show menu bar**.

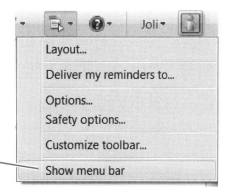

If you want your Menu Bar back permanently, this is the option for you.

The reading pane is on the right now too, but are you used to Outlook Express? If you are and you want to put the reading pane back where it belongs, underneath the message list:

→ Click the Menus button and then **Layout**. You'll find options here to return the reading pane to the position you're used to.

→ Other layout options you can change include customizing the Menu Bar.

Did you have a color scheme set up for your e-mail? Want to recreate it? There are a couple of new icons on the **Command bar** that allow you to change the color of the interface and access familiar menu options. It'd be in your best interest to explore those too.

→ Click the **Colorizer** button to choose a color that better suits your tastes.

The colorizer button is a paintbrush, what else?!

What about spam?

Do you want to limit the amount of spam you get? To fight harder against spam, click the Menus icon and then **Safety Options**. Try the **High** option to reduce the volume of spam you get.

Make sure to check the Junk e-mail folder frequently for a while, though, because you'll need to "train" Windows Live Mail as to what's junk and what isn't.

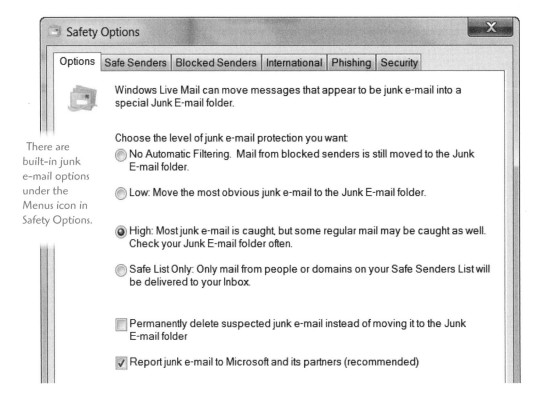

There are built-in junk e-mail options under the Menus icon in Safety Options.

Take a break

Take a break and walk around. Grab a drink, read a magazine article, or even go for a short walk. Give your brain about 10 minutes' break then come back here for the Review and the Experiment. It doesn't matter what you do, and it sounds counterintuitive, but try not to actively think about what you just learned and your brain will take care of the rest!

Review

You learned a lot in this chapter about Windows Live Mail and a little about networking. Because you don't set up new networks very often, it's highly probable that the next time you do, you'll have to refer to this book and the notes you took during this chapter to do it again. You've already done a mini review for connecting to the Internet, so let's review Windows Live Mail here.

↺ Which of the following did you install along with Mail?

☐ Messenger

☐ Photo Gallery

☐ Toolbar

☐ Writer

☐ Family Safety

↺ Windows Live Mail has a lot in common with previous e-mail programs (like Outlook Express/Windows Mail/Microsoft Office Outlook/other):

→ Create accounts for multiple .... and access all of them from a single interface.

→ You can still .... the Inbox to create a new folder.

→ A Junk e-mail filter that can be found in the .... menu.

→ An Options dialog box is available from the .... menu.

→ You can .... the folder data by From, Subject, Date, Sent, and other familiar headings.

↺ Windows Live Mail is different than your previous e-mail program:

→ .... has replaced Send/Receive.

→ There are two new buttons on the Toolbar: Launch the .... and ....

How did you do?

If you'd like to improve your recall on any of these you should spend a little more time on that part of the chapter. You'll get more familiar with the new information faster if you take a little time to make some strong links to the new information you're learning.

Experiment

The best way to really cement these features and techniques into your long-term memory is to expand on the techniques you learned in the chapter by using them and taking them just one step further.

Here are some suggestions for your experiment using techniques covered in this chapter.

Make your e-mails stand out!

Do you want your e-mail to really stand out? Do you want to format the text with different font sizes, fonts, and colors? Would you like to add stationery? And what about misspelled words, wouldn't it be great if you never had to worry about typos ever again? You can do all of this and more with Windows Live Mail.

Here are some of the things you can do while composing a new message or replying to or forwarding one you've received:

→ Mail's new, **inline spell check** feature will automatically correct common capitalization and spelling mistakes. Change the settings or turn off inline spell check from the Menus icon. Click Options, and in the Options dialog box, choose the Spelling tab.

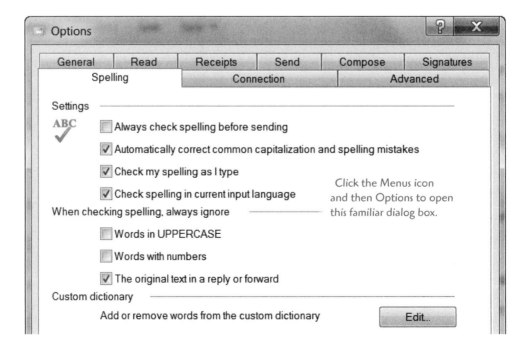

Click the Menus icon and then Options to open this familiar dialog box.

→ Mail has **Format** and **Stationery** options built right into all outgoing e-mail messages. Click the Format button (next to Add photos), and apply the formatting options as desired.

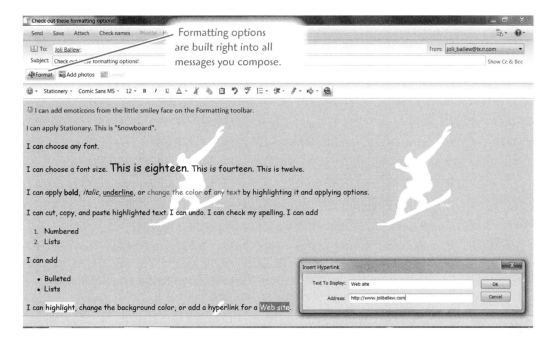

Calendaring

If you couldn't help but notice the new **Add to calendar** option in Windows Live Mail, and the **Calendar icon** at the bottom of the Folder pane, and you needed to schedule some time to look into it, you're in luck.

Click Calendar at the bottom of the Folder window. What happens?

Say you need to add a lunch date next Thursday. You need to create a new calendar event or appointment, but how?

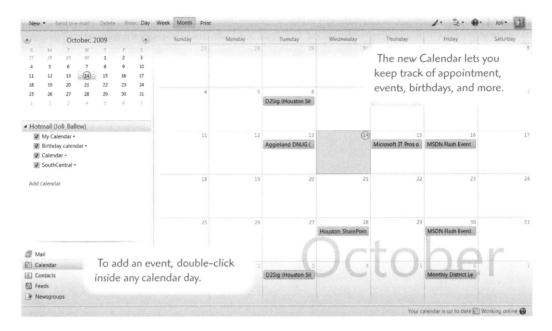

The new Calendar lets you keep track of appointment, events, birthdays, and more.

To add an event, double-click inside any calendar day.

Double-click inside any calendar day. Doesn't the window that opens look a lot like a new e-mail? Fill in the information for the subject, location, start and end times for your lunch date. Do you want Mail to send you a reminder? Set it up here. Click the Menus icon to state where to send those reminders to. You can opt for an e-mail to your Live address, a mobile device, or even have the reminder sent to you via Live Messenger. When you're finished, click Save & Close. Where does the new item appear?

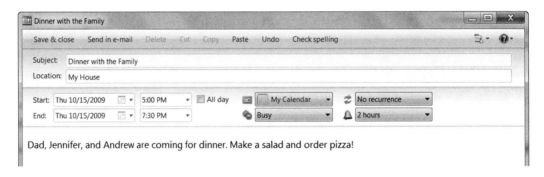

Here are some other things to try:

→ Add a calendar event from an e-mail.
While you're reading a mail that needs a calendar entry, click Add to calendar to create a new "event." The e-mail is inserted in the event automatically, and you configure the dates and times.

→ Add a new calendar for another member of your family or one for your sport training sessions. Click Add calendar. Name the calendar and pick a calendar color to differentiate the entries in the calendar.

→ Add others' calendars to yours by subscribing to them. You can choose from public calendars or calendars others have shared.

→ Access and share a calendar online.

Any calendar you create or manage in Windows Live Mail on your PC is synchronized automatically with the calendar feature on your Windows Live home page when you're connected to the Internet. Don't believe it? Create a few events in Windows Live Mail using the Calendar feature on your computer, and then go to www.windowslive.com and log in.

Once you're logged in, click More, and click Calendar. Hover your mouse over any event you created on your PC. You'll see it here too!

If you created a calendar for your sport training sessions, wouldn't it be great if you could share it with your family so they know when you're going to be away from the phone? Click Share. Choose the calendar to share (if you have more than one, you can, of course, share your main calendar). Don't worry—you have complete control over how your calendar is shared. Click Share this Calendar and choose how to share and with whom.

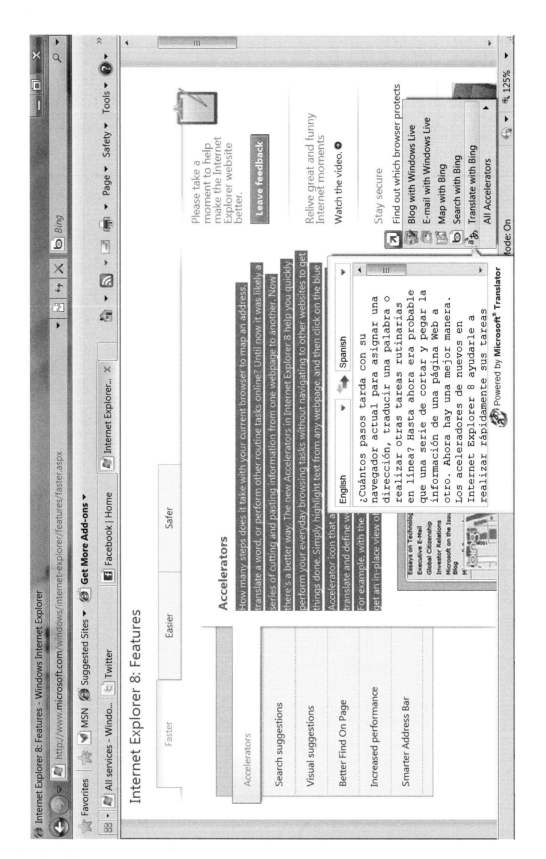

3 Is surfing the Web the same as before?

So you're online, connected to your home network, and your e-mail's all set up. But when you click the familiar big blue 'e' to check out what's happening on Facebook, it turns out Internet Explorer is different too! Although surfing still works the same way it always did, the new version has some new features that can help you save time, but only once you've found your way around and answered a few pretty big questions.

⇨ Where have all the toolbars gone?

⇨ What does "tabbed browsing" mean?

⇨ When would you need to use Compatibility view?

⇨ Which multiple search providers should you add?

⇨ What are Accelerators and Web Slices, and how does they work?

No Problem!

Most of the new features help you do what you need to do on the Net, faster. Now you can:

⇨ Get a map of an address with a mouse click.

⇨ Translate an entire Web page into another language.

⇨ Search from the Search box using very specific providers, like Amazon, eBay, or ESPN.

⇨ Get up to date information on stuff like your local weather right from the Internet Explorer toolbar.

But first things first. Who moved your Menu Bar and how do you get it back?

Show the Menu Bar

Where's the **Menu Bar** that had File, Edit, View, Favorites, Tools, and Help? Where are the Explorer bars, like History and Feeds? And where are Internet Options? Don't panic. It's all still there; hold tight!

Microsoft has hidden the Menu Bar on purpose, to get you to move toward friendlier icons and menus. But if you like the toolbar, you can still use it. Press Alt. What happens?

Yep, that's all there is to getting your **Menu Bar** back. Now that the Menu bar's showing, you can access all of your menus and familiar features, like Tools > Internet Options and your Favorites list.

The menus are still there, you just have to press Alt to get to the Menu Bar first!

Make a link

Press **Alt** for an **[Alt]ernative** view of Internet Explorer.

Do you want the Menu Bar to show *permanently*? Don't press anything on the keyboard this time. Instead, right-click where the Menu Bar should be, and click on Menu Bar in the pop-up menu. What happens to the menu item when you click it?

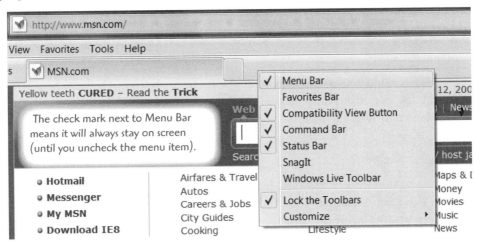

Do you like the minimal look without the Menu Bar, but wonder if you will still be able to access all the familiar options? Do you see the Safety and Tools icons? They're located to the right of the Home icon and work the same way they always have.

Click the Page icon. If you've previously used the options to zoom in or out, or change the text size, this is where you find those options in the new Internet Explorer. But what are those other options?

Play with it

Explore the Internet Explorer icons, menus, and Favorites button, and find out what other features are available, and where, and discover a few new options along the way.

1. Press Alt on the keyboard to show the Menu Bar (if it's not showing right now). Click **Tools > Internet Options**. In the Internet Options dialog box, click the **Security** tab. Check your security settings are how you like them. Medium or Medium-High should be good choices for most people.

   On the **Command Bar**—that's the bar with the Home, Page, Safety, and Tools options—click **Tools**. This is another way to access your Internet Options.

2. If you like to **delete your temporary Internet files**, cookies, or History, click **Tools** on the Command Bar and choose your option.

    Now, on the Command Bar, click **Safety**. Notice that Delete Browsing History is an option there, too.

3. How do you add something you like to the **Favorites list**? **Click the yellow star** on the Command bar to add a favorite, or for a more familiar way show the Menu Bar, click Favorites > Add to Favorites.

    While you're here on the Favorites Bar, click Suggested Sites. Do any of the suggestions appeal?

4. Do you want to **import** favorites, feeds, and cookies from another browser? Show the Menu Bar again, click File. Which option would you use to import and export your favorites?

5. Do you want to **search** for specific words or phrases on a web page? On the Menu Bar, click Edit > Find on this page.

6. From the Command Bar, click **Page**. Note that there are options for Blog with Windows Live, E-mail with Windows Live, Translate with Bing and more. These tasks can also be achieved using Accelerators, which you'll see in a moment. What other options are listed under Page that you'd use? How and why would you use them?

Set multiple home pages to open automatically in tabs

Most everyone visits the same pages every time they surf the Internet. When you open Internet Explorer do you routinely open a window to do any of the following?

→ Log in to your Facebook, MySpace, or Twitter account.

→ Check the sports scores from the night before.

→ Read the news on your favorite news page?

→ Get your favorite search engine ready?

→ Maybe even all of these . . .

We're all creatures of habit, but navigating to all those pages manually, or even accessing them from your list of Favorites, takes time. Wouldn't it be great if you could save the time it takes to open all your "everyday" pages every time you open Internet Explorer?

The easiest way to have all these pages open as soon as you open Internet Explorer is to configure multiple web pages as home pages. How does that work?

Try it out. Let's start by opening all your favorites in tabs. In what? If you're not familiar with tabbed browsing, it's simply a way to keep multiple web pages open at the same time in the same window, without opening multiple Internet Explorer windows.

Go to your first favorite page, then instead of opening another window, **press Ctrl+T**. What happens to your browser window? It *looks* like you're in a new window, except you're in the same window as your first favorite. You can switch between the pages using the tabs at the top of their windows. See them? Open a new tab for each of your favorite everyday pages.

Once you've opened all your favorite pages in a set of tabs, click the **arrow** next to the **Home** button. Click **Add or Change Home Page**, and then click **Use the current tab set as your home page**. Quit Internet Explorer then start it up again. What do you see? Right, Internet Explorer opens a window with these same tabs already open.

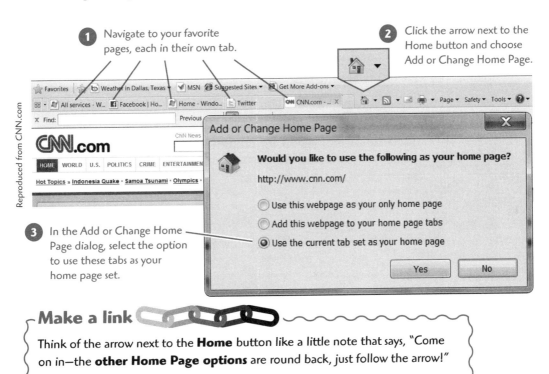

1 Navigate to your favorite pages, each in their own tab.

2 Click the arrow next to the Home button and choose Add or Change Home Page.

Reproduced from CNN.com

3 In the Add or Change Home Page dialog, select the option to use these tabs as your home page set.

Add or Change Home Page

Would you like to use the following as your home page?

http://www.cnn.com/

○ Use this webpage as your only home page
○ Add this webpage to your home page tabs
● Use the current tab set as your home page

Yes   No

Make a link

Think of the arrow next to the **Home** button like a little note that says, "Come on in—the **other Home Page options** are round back, just follow the arrow!"

Use Web Slices to access information that changes often

Say you're surfing the Web and you realize you're late for a meeting. You need to check the local traffic before you run out the door. How would you check the traffic real quick?

If you said you'd use Peek to check a gadget on your Desktop, that would work provided the gadget that offers that information exists. If there's no gadget you can add, you're going to have to hunt down and navigate to a website and that takes time. Wouldn't it be great if you could save *just the bit of the traffic site that gives you local traffic information* for next time?

What you need is a **Web Slice**. **Web Slices** let you get updated information on weather, news, stock prices, sports scores, traffic, and more, right from Internet Explorer's Favorites bar.

Because Web Slices are so new, not many sites offer them yet, and a lot of Web Slice information crosses over with what gadgets offer, it might take a while to get on board with Web Slices. However, for information for which no gadgets exist, a Web slice with the desired information can save you a whole load of time.

Are you looking for movie times for the theater down the street, show times for a local community center, TV listings for specific cable channels, and up-to-the-minute sports scores from websites like ESPN? This is the kind of information Web Slices were made for, but how do you know if a site offers Web Slices?

1. In Internet Explorer, perform a search at `www.Bing.com` for "Weather" followed by a major city close to where you live.

2. Move your mouse over the results. Do you see a green accelerator icon next to the results? That means a Web Slice is available.

Search for your local weather. If a green accelerator icon appears when you move the cursor near the results, that means a Web Slice is available.

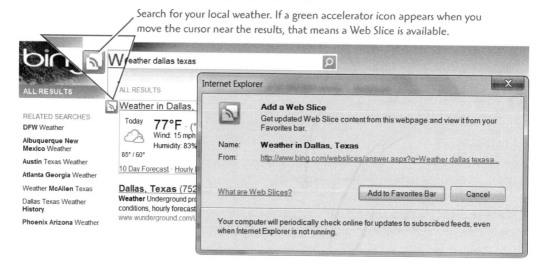

3. Click the icon and when prompted, click **Add to Favorites Bar**.

4. How do you check your Web Slice? Click the new **Web Slice** icon on your Favorites Bar and the slice of the page that has the latest weather for your area appears.

Play with it

Find another Web Slice. Do you have time to do random searches "just in case" a page in the results offers slices? If you do, knock yourself out, but if you don't, visit www. ieaddons.com. Scroll down to the bottom of the page to the Internet Explorer 8 only section. Click the Web Slices link. Here are some Web Slices you can try:

→ Traffic from Bing

→ ESPN Sports

→ New York Times Latest Headlines

→ Finance from Bing

Make a link

Get Internet takeout: save the most useful bits of pages as delicious **Web Slices** you can enjoy later.

Get faster and better search results

Searching works the same in the new version of Internet Explorer as it always did. Type your keywords or question into any search engine (or the Search bar in your browser window) and press Enter. But how often have you searched for something, visited a web page from the results and only found once you're there that the page wasn't at all what you needed? How much time would it save if you could preview the pages from the search results first, or just search a specific site without having to visit it first?

Internet Explorer 8 lets you perform website-specific searches. Say you want to search www.Amazon.com for a specific product, www.eBay.com for a hard to find item, or even www.Wikipedia.org for information about an obscure word. How much time would you save if you could search those sites without navigating to them first?

1. Add search providers

Click the arrow next to the Search window in Internet Explorer then click **Find More Providers**. What happens?

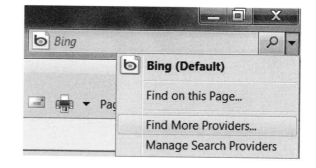

Browse the gallery of providers you could add. What are your interests? What do you generally search for? If it's sports you like, try ESPN Search, if it's news, try New York Times Instant Search.

Each time you add a search provider you'll be asked if you want to make it your default provider. What do you think will happen if you do?

Making a site your default search provider means every search you perform will use that provider. Good if your provider is ESPN and you're searching for sports news; not so hot if you want international financial news. How would you choose another provider or go back to Bing if you prefer a general search engine?

Click the arrow next to the Search window in Internet Explorer again and choose the **Manage Search Providers option** from the drop-down list.

2. Search using a specific provider

So you've added some new search providers like ESPN, Amazon, or the New York Times but how do you search using your new providers? There are two ways:

1. Click the arrow next to the Search window to select an alternate provider *before* you type any keywords. What happens to the provider listed in the window?

Here's Yahoo set as the current search engine.

Anything you type in the Search window now will provide results from Yahoo! only. You can view the results in a drop-down list without having to visit the Yahoo! site. If you see something you like, click the link in the list to navigate to that page.

2. This time around type your keywords into the window *first*, then click the arrow in the Search window. Select any provider from the list. What happens this time?

    Instead of showing a list of results in the preview window, your browser takes you to the page that contains the results search on the provider's website.

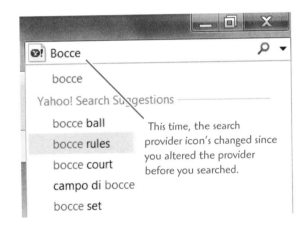

This time, the search provider icon's changed since you altered the provider before you searched.

Which option do you prefer? Why? Is one option better for certain kinds of results? Why?

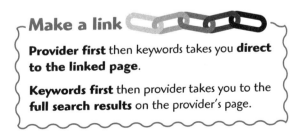

Make a link

Provider first then keywords takes you **direct to the linked page**.

Keywords first then provider takes you to the **full search results** on the provider's page.

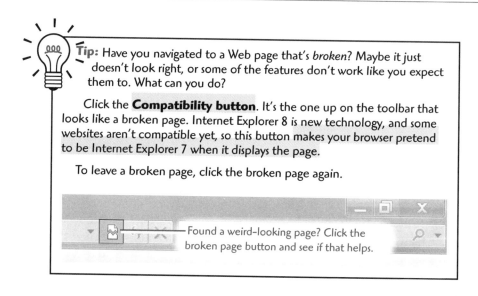

Tip: Have you navigated to a Web page that's *broken*? Maybe it just doesn't look right, or some of the features don't work like you expect them to. What can you do?

Click the **Compatibility button**. It's the one up on the toolbar that looks like a broken page. Internet Explorer 8 is new technology, and some websites aren't compatible yet, so this button makes your browser pretend to be Internet Explorer 7 when it displays the page.

To leave a broken page, click the broken page again.

Found a weird-looking page? Click the broken page button and see if that helps.

More information in fewer clicks

There are other ways that Internet Explorer 8 can help you speed up everyday tasks. Say you want to e-mail your friends to invite them to Happy Hour at your local bar, or post an invite on Facebook. Think of the steps it takes:

1. Do a Web search for the pub's address:
   a. Highlight the address.
   b. Copy the address.

2. Open a new tab and type in the address of a mapping page like MapQuest or Google Maps:
   a. Paste the address in the Search window.
   b. Click Get Map or Search Maps to get the map you're looking for.

3. Find some option for sending the map and the address in an e-mail. You may or may not find an option to send the information to Facebook (even if you have the Facebook bookmarklet enabled, that's still another click).

That's a lot of clicking for a very small amount of information. You just want to have Happy Hour, and you'd like to do it sometime today. You need a better way . . .

Internet Explorer 8 feels your pain and so **Accelerators** were born. **Accelerators** let you do things like this with minimal clicking.

Try it for yourself. Highlight text you want to map and share (or translate, or send via e-mail, or search for) on any web page. Do you see the Accelerator icon appear above or underneath it? You can see the icon here; it looks like an arrow.

What happens when you click the Accelerator icon?

What do you think each of these options does?

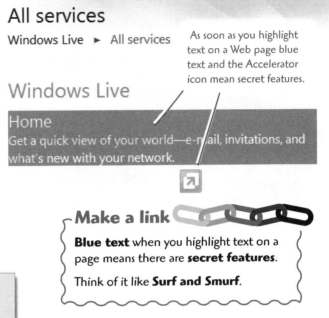

All services

Windows Live ► All services

As soon as you highlight text on a Web page blue text and the Accelerator icon mean secret features.

Windows Live

Home
Get a quick view of your world—e-mail, invitations, and what's new with your network.

Make a link

Blue text when you highlight text on a page means there are **secret features**.

Think of it like **Surf and Smurf**.

Try one and see if you were right. Find a page with a street address on it, highlight the address, click the accelerator icon and choose the Map with Bing option.

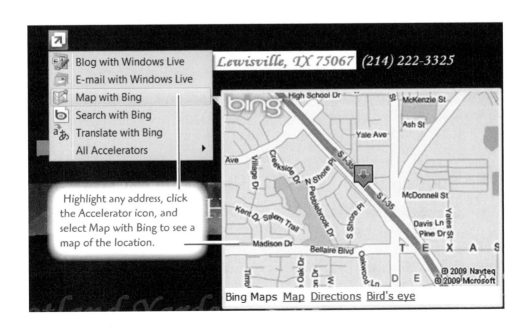

Highlight any address, click the Accelerator icon, and select Map with Bing to see a map of the location.

Will all of the options work regardless of the type of text you select? Click any item in the list to make that command happen.

Can you find more Accelerators or manage the ones you already have?

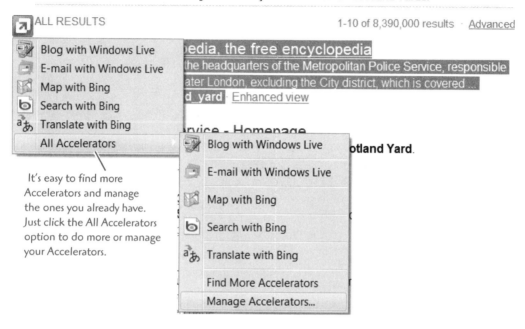

Results are included for scotland **yard**. Show just the results for Scotland Yards.

It's easy to find more Accelerators and manage the ones you already have. Just click the All Accelerators option to do more or manage your Accelerators.

Play with it

Use Accelerators to plan your Happy Hour in super-quick time. Go ahead and do a search for any listing that offers an address for your favorite pub.

The Boot and Saddle Club - Nevada Thing To Do

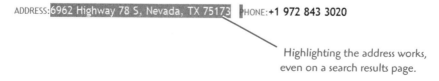

ADDRESS:6962 Highway 78 S, Nevada, TX 75173 PHONE:+1 972 843 3020

Highlighting the address works, even on a search results page.

Click the Accelerator icon. What happens when you hover your cursor over Bing Maps? Use this method to make sure that the map displays the location you want.

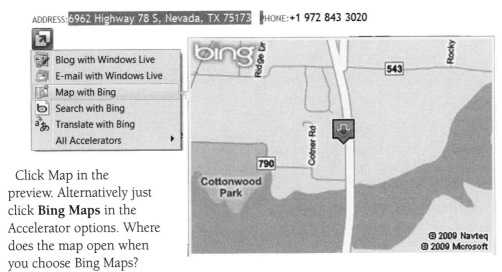

Click Map in the preview. Alternatively just click **Bing Maps** in the Accelerator options. Where does the map open when you choose Bing Maps?

Do you see the option to Share on the new map page? Opt to send the map in an e-mail, add a little note about meeting for Happy Hour (or dinner), and you've got yourself a party!

- -

Take a break

Your brain needs time to sift through what you just learned about Internet Explorer 8. Time to take a break. We're nearly at the end of the chapter. All that's left is an Experiment or two. So, walk away and give your brain something else to focus on for just a little while.

Review

Use this space to write down what you remember about showing the Menu Bar, opening web pages in tabs, setting multiple Home pages to open automatically, Web Slices, adding and using Search providers, and Accelerators.

↺ Find the Internet Options dialog box via the .... icon on the Command Bar or by pressing the .... key.

↺ You can delete your browsing History and cookies via the .... icon and also the Tools ....

↺ To open a new tab, press .... + ... on your keyboard.

↺ Open all your favorite pages in multiple tabs in one window. To make the same tabs to open every time you start Internet Explorer, click the arrow next to the .... icon then add the tabbed group.

↺ Web Slices allow you to get .... on many ever-changing topics like: Weather, News, Sports scores, and Traffic.

↺ You can search a specific website (like Amazon) without navigating to it by adding a ....

↺ You can change your .... search provider from Bing to a provider of your choice.

↺ Choose a different provider from the list .... typing any keywords to return results from

....

↺ Access search results on a .... provided by a specific provider (like Google or Yahoo!) by typing .... then clicking the arrow to choose a different provider.

↺ Accelerators let you do the following with selected text:

1. .... to your Windows Live Space.

2. E-mail with ....

3. .... a location.

4. .... for more information.

5. .... the page to another language.

How did you do?

If you'd like to improve your recall on any of these you should go spend a little more time on that part of the chapter.

Experiment

The best way to really cement these features and techniques into your long-term memory is to expand on the techniques you learned in the chapter by using them and taking them just one step further.

Here are some suggestions for your experiment using techniques covered in this chapter.

Find more Accelerators

To find more accelerators, highlight any text and click All Accelerators, then pause on Find More Accelerators. Browse through the available accelerators and select the ones you like to use. The new accelerator is added to your All Accelerators list. Current options are:

- → Share on Facebook
- → Send with Windows Live Hotmail
- → Google Define
- → Define Acronym
- → Share on Twitter
- → Bing Image Search

Manage your Accelerators

What if you've got so many Accelerators listed that you can't find the one you're looking for—can you delete Accelerators from the list? Click **All Accelerators**, then choose **Manage Accelerators**.

Start your own blog

You know that one of the Accelerators in Internet Explorer is Blog with Windows Live. All you need to get started blogging is a Live ID, which you may already have. (If you don't have a Live ID and you'd like to start a blog, check chapter 1 to see how to get one).

Find something on the Internet that interests you. It could be a news headline, information about a sports team you like, or perhaps even something about a health issue, like diabetes. Select the text, and click the Accelerator to blog. What happens?

Your first blog post will look a lot like an e-mail, while editing it at least. Edit the blog as desired and click Publish. The blog entry will appear on your Live home page. From there, you can add more blogs, add a comment, and even invite people to read your blog posts.

Manage your photos

You've got digital photos everywhere:

⇨ On a digital camera.

⇨ On an old computer.

⇨ On SD cards.

⇨ On a CD your kids gave you.

⇨ And what about that box of old photos you'd like to scan and preserve?

You need to consolidate, backup, and organize. You'd also like an easy option for posting your favorite photos on the Web. But how? And where is the Windows 7 photo-editing program, anyway? It doesn't look like it comes with one.

No Problem!

There's no pre-installed photo-editing program in Windows 7, but the Windows Live Essentials suite has a free application that does exactly what you need.

Windows Live Photo Gallery will let you:

⇨ Import pictures from a camera, SD card, or scanner right from the interface.

⇨ Edit to your heart's content.

⇨ Create folders and organize your pictures in them, and include folders from other networked computers in the gallery.

⇨ Upload your favorite photos to your Windows Live personalized web page.

Do you have Windows Live Photo Gallery?

Do you remember if you installed Windows Live Photo Gallery in chapter 2? Take a look in the All Programs list under Windows Live, do you see it?

Note: If you do have Windows Live Photo Gallery, you're good to go on to the next section, at the bottom of the next page.

If you've already installed your digital camera *and* imported some pictures, you can skip forward even further to the editing section (on page 68).

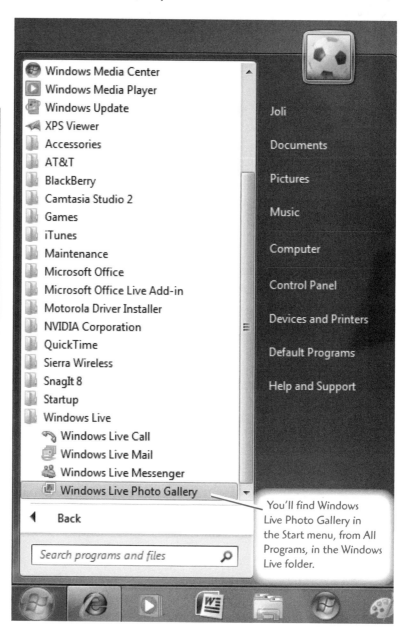

You'll find Windows Live Photo Gallery in the Start menu, from All Programs, in the Windows Live folder.

If you don't have Windows Live Photo Gallery, you'll need to get it:

1. In Internet Explorer go to `http://download.live.com`.

2. Click Photo Gallery and click Download.

From your camera to the web

With Photo Gallery, it's a snap to get your photos and videos from your camera to your PC. Find your favorite photos and share them with friends and family. Make your great photos look even better, and create impressive panoramic photos too.

Get Photo Gallery, or all these programs—they're free!

Choose your language:

English (English)

Clicking "Download" means you agree to the Microsoft service agreement and privacy statement. The download may include updates to Windows Live programs you already have. You'll get future updates to these and other Microsoft programs from Microsoft Update. Learn more

Download

System requirements

Programs you can download include:

Messenger
Mail
Writer
Photo Gallery
Movie Maker
Family Safety
Toolbar

Windows Live Photo Gallery is an all-in-one photo management and editing solution.

3. You may be prompted to log into Windows Live the first time you use Windows Live Photo Gallery.

Import pictures from a digital device

If you've taken some great pictures but never uploaded them to your PC for viewing and sharing, you're not alone. If you often require your friends to hover around your cell phone to look at the pictures you took with it, you're not alone there either. C'mon, no one *really* wants to look at your cell phone or camera window to see your pictures!

There are more good reasons for importing photos from your digital camera or phone; you don't want to accidentally write over any pictures, lose them or the SD card they're stored on, or worse, have your camera stolen after returning from a once-in-a-lifetime vacation.

Once the pictures are on the PC, you can do all kinds of things with them:

→ Print them at home.

→ Copy your favorites to an SD card and print them from a drugstore kiosk.

→ View them on the PC in a slide show.

→ Send the pictures in a regular e-mail or a photo e-mail with Windows Live Mail.

→ Post them to your personal or work website.

→ Post them to a social networking site.

→ Post them to your free Windows Live home page—the one you got when you obtained your Windows Live ID.

→ Burn a DVD others can watch on their computers or DVD players.

How else could you share your photos? Perhaps you could create a slideshow using Microsoft Office PowerPoint for a birthday party, graduation, or roast? Maybe you want to create a photo book using an online printing company. What other ways can you share photos?

Get the pictures off the device and onto the PC

The most common way to pull photos off a device is to connect the camera to the PC and install it. Once it's installed, you can view and manage the pictures just about any way you'd like. If your camera or phone has an SD card, you don't even have to install the device. Just remove the card and insert it into a media card slot on the PC. Almost all PCs these days come with a compatible card reader, so if your photos are on an SD card, this the most efficient way to import them.

> **Note:** In the next two sections you'll learn how to upload pictures from a media card and from a camera or phone. If you can, follow the steps for the *media card*. When you copy pictures from a media card you don't have to install any software, but if you want to transfer photos from a camera or phone, you sometimes do have to install software.
>
> So, if software's easier to install in Windows 7, why avoid installing new software?
>
> Much of the software you're asked to install when you install from the CD or DVD that came with your camera or phone is software you don't need, like picture viewers and editors. You have Windows Live Photo Gallery; that's all you need.

Import pictures from a media card

Does your digital camera or cell phone use an SD card? Does your computer have an SD card slot that's compatible (or a card reader plugged into your computer)? If you have an SD card and an SD card reader, you're in luck because the easiest way to copy the images on the card to the PC is to insert the card into the media card slot.

1. Insert your SD card the card reader.

   a. Built-in media card reader

   b. USB media card reader

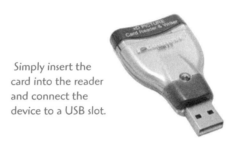

   Simply insert the card into the reader and connect the device to a USB slot.

2. After you insert the card into a media card slot on the PC, you'll see a prompt to copy the images. Select **Import pictures and videos using Windows Live Photo Gallery**.

   In the second window choose **Import all new items now**, and give the group of pictures a descriptive name. Click Import. You can try out the more advanced options later.

After you insert a media card from a digital camera or phone, you'll be prompted to import the images and/or videos it contains. Choose the Windows Live Photo Gallery option.

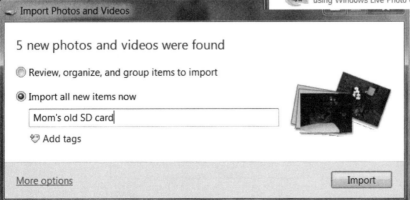

What happens after the upload process completes? Are you able to see the photos easily? Are they in a specific folder?

Install a digital camera

If your digital camera doesn't have a media card, or your computer doesn't have a card reader, you'll have to install the device to pull the pictures off it and get them on your PC. To do that:

1. Make sure your digital camera is *switched off*, then connect the camera to your PC with the cables provided with the camera. Often, one end is quite small and the other is USB.

2. Turn on the camera.

3. Wait while the device installs. Almost always, installation happens automatically, but if it doesn't, try inserting the CD that came with the camera and installing from there.

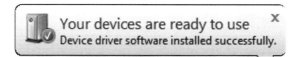

4. Once the camera's installed, you'll be prompted to import pictures. Select **Import pictures and videos using Windows Live Photo Gallery.**

Play with it

Install an iPhone, BlackBerry, or similar device. If you were prompted to insert a CD or DVD or install another program after connecting your camera phone to your PC, you'll want to do that to get all of the available features. iPhones require iTunes; BlackBerry smartphones require the BlackBerry Desktop Software or BlackBerry Media Sync; and even media players (like Zune) require specialized software to work properly. Find out what software you need by visiting the manufacturer's website to download and install it.

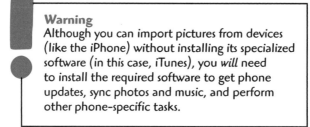

Warning
Although you can import pictures from devices (like the iPhone) without installing its specialized software (in this case, iTunes), you *will* need to install the required software to get phone updates, sync photos and music, and perform other phone-specific tasks.

Get pictures stored on other PCs

Do you have another PC with digital pictures on it that you want to consolidate, view, manage, and organize in your new photo library? What's the best way to do that?

When you set up a new PC, it's a good idea to get everything into one folder and create subfolders to organize the data, so you can manage those pictures as one unit. If your new PC has lots of free hard drive space and you have a reliable backup system in place, it's an even more attractive option. You can opt to copy or to move the data as you like.

Copy or move

You already know how to **move** and **copy** data over a network. To simply *copy* the photos, open two windows (old PC on the left, Pictures Library on your Windows 7 PC on the right), select the photos on the old PC, right-click and choose **Copy**, then navigate to the new location (in the other window), right-click and choose **Paste**.

To *move* the photos, choose **Cut** instead of Copy. You can also drag the files to the new location, as shown here. (Use Snap to position the two windows for dragging!)

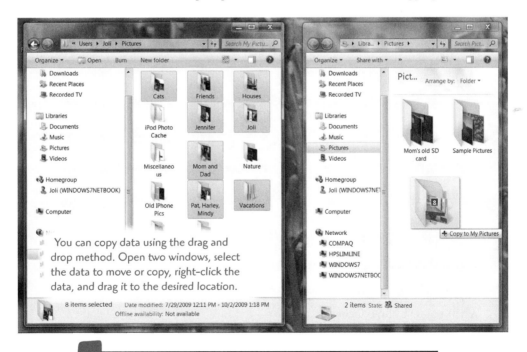

You can copy data using the drag and drop method. Open two windows, select the data to move or copy, right–click the data, and drag it to the desired location.

STOP! However you do it, be sure to import, move, or copy some pictures now, so you'll have some personal pictures to work with in this chapter.

Use photos over a network

What if you don't want to move the pictures to your new PC or create a copy of them? What are your options? There's one more way to deal with photos stored on other PCs. You can add the My Pictures folder on an older Windows XP machine, or the Pictures folder on a Vista or Windows 7 PC as a **network folder** to the Windows Live Photo Gallery on your new PC.

Tip: You can't add a folder from a PC that's turned off, which makes moving or copying the data a more desirable option.

1. From Windows Live Photo Gallery's **File** menu, click **Include a folder in the gallery…** .

   If you click File and don't see the option to include a folder in the gallery, click the Back to gallery button and try again.

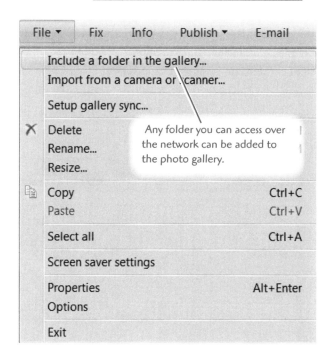

Any folder you can access over the network can be added to the photo gallery.

2. Browse to the folder that holds your pictures on the networked machine.

3. Click OK. Where do the pictures appear?

   When you tell Photo Gallery to add a folder, you'll be able to view the items in that folder as if they were on the PC itself.

Make a link

Photo Gallery is laid out a lot like Windows Explorer. If you're having trouble navigating the pictures and picture folders, compare Windows Live Photo Gallery's interface side by side with the Windows Explorer window. Windows Live Photo Gallery works the same as Windows Explorer. Expand or collapse folders to view or hide their contents, and view thumbnails or auto arrange the icons.

The Live Photo Gallery folders are organized the same way Windows Explorer folders are. Photo Gallery is shown on the left; Windows Explorer on the right.

Play with it

Now that you've imported, moved, copied, or can access some photos over the network, there are some additional familiar options to explore:

→ Right-click an empty area of the Photo Gallery window and click **View** to change what it displays. Try the Thumbnails with file name option. Would another option—date taken, date modified, rating, caption, or size—work better for you? Try it and see if you're right.

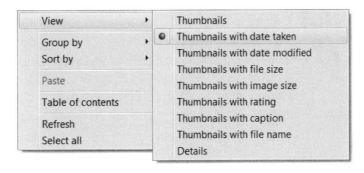

→ Just like other Microsoft programs (like Windows Live Mail), some folders are automatically created to sort and filter data. In the left pane click Date taken. What do you think sorting by Descriptive tags will do to your pictures?

→ Hover your cursor over any image without actually selecting it to get a pop-up with more information about the image. This works the same way with items in Explorer windows.

→ Right-click any item to view the usual Explorer options including Set as desktop background, Copy, Delete, Rename, and more. There are some right-click options that are specific to Photo Gallery including Resize, Rotate clockwise, Rotate counterclockwise, and Clear rating.

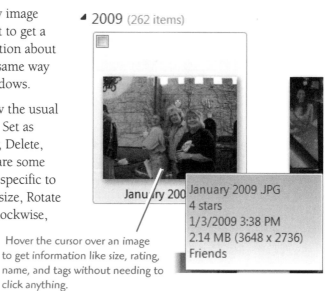

◢ 2009 (262 items)

January 2009 JPG
4 stars
1/3/2009 3:38 PM
2.14 MB (3648 x 2736)
Friends

Hover the cursor over an image to get information like size, rating, name, and tags without needing to click anything.

Get organized

Do you have pictures from a bunch of different places and events in your Pictures Library now? Do you want to organize them? Before you do anything drastic, make a list of the things and events you've taken pictures of. Do you have pictures from vacations, weddings, graduations, cities, or kids? Perhaps you have lots of pictures of pets. Make a list here:

....
....
....
....
....
....
....

Open the Pictures folder and **create a subfolder** for each of the subjects you just listed. Create subfolders inside of your subfolders if you need to. Here the Cats subfolder has a few of subfolders of its own. When your folders are ready, select and then copy (or cut) the photos you want to move in the main Pictures Library, navigate to the appropriate folder, and paste the photos there.

Create subfolders and subfolders inside of them. Move pictures into their proper folders to get organized.

Alternatively, since your camera or phone saved the details of the date each photo was taken, you can click **Arrange by Dates** in the Navigation pane to list your photos by the date they were taken.

Finally, browse the pictures you already have. Do any need to be rotated? Do you have a favorite you'd like to use as your Desktop Background? If so:

1. Right-click any photo that needs to be rotated and choose **Rotate** (in either direction).

2. Find a picture you want to use as your Desktop background. Right-click it and choose **Set as desktop background**.

You can also set Windows Live Photo Gallery to "watch" a folder. Learn more about this in chapter 9.

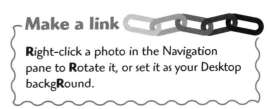

Make a link

Right-click a photo in the Navigation pane to **R**otate it, or set it as your Desktop backg**R**ound.

Edit your pictures

You've imported, added, moved, or copied your photos, and your Windows Live Photo Gallery's shaping up. But there's a problem. Now that you can see them on a bigger monitor, you can tell that some of those pictures don't look nearly as good as they did on your tiny cell phone screen. Your photos need a few fixes, but how will you do that?

Windows Live Photo Gallery gives you easy-to-use editing tools for just this kind of situation. Let's take a look.

Play with it

1. Open Windows Live Photo Gallery and double-click a picture that needs editing.

2. In the resulting window, click **Fix**.

    There are a few options in here. The ones you're most likely to need include Auto Adjust, Straighten Photo, Crop Photo, and Fix Red Eye.

    Explore the options including:

    → **Auto Adjust**, which makes Windows Live Photo Gallery apply adjustments automatically. These adjustments include straightening, brightness, contrast, and more. (Note the Undo button appears after performing this adjustment.)

    → **Straighten photo**, which lets you manually straighten the photo using a slider. Use this when auto adjust doesn't do the job. You can also use it for effect—to slant something not normally slanted.

    → **Crop photo**, which removes unnecessary parts of a photo. Auto Adjust won't crop a photo for you, so use Crop in conjunction with Auto Adjust to perfect a photo.

    → **Fix red eye**, which allows you to manually select red eyes but removes the red color automatically.

Make a link

Auto adjust = A quick fix, **auto**matically!

If all the ocean's tipping out of a photo, you better straighten it, quick!

During harvest, a farmer cuts his **crop** and *keeps only the useful part.*

Do you know what causes **red eye**? It's the light of the flash reflecting off the red blood vessels in the eye. No one wants to see that. Ewww! Better **fix** it fast.

Do you want to save your original photo before you start messing with it? *Changes are saved by default* when you click the **Back to gallery** button. But you can choose **File > Make a copy** to save the changes under another file name. But what if you already made some changes and you clicked Back to gallery and your changes have been saved; can you undo the changes? Don't worry, all is not lost! You can always choose **File > Revert to original** if you change your mind.

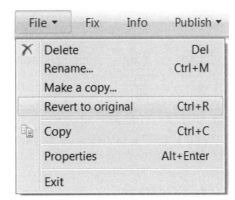

Share your photos

You've got well-organized and beautifully edited photos and now you want to share them with the world, but how will you do that? Windows Live Photo Gallery offers the usual way to share photos, including the option to e-mail and print right from the toolbar.

There are other ways to share photos, all built in to the Photo Gallery interface. Let's start with a simple one. Say you want to display your favorite photos as a screensaver, but you've got more than one favorite photo, how will you show more than one? Try:

☐ **File > Screen saver settings** to configure a screen saver with your favorite photos.

Do you want to upload photos to your Windows Live website? Your Windows Live ID gives you your own free, personalized website. Select a few photos and click **Publish**, then **Online album** to upload them to your website. Choose the picture size and who to share with. Click Publish.

Once uploaded, you'll be able to view the images on the Internet, no matter where you are!

☐ Choose **Publish > Group album** to send selected photos to a group you belong to on Windows Live. (You can also create a new group during the process.)

☐ Choose **Publish > Event Album** to send selected photos to an event album you've created.

What if you don't have a Windows Live Web page and you prefer to share your photos via other social networking accounts like Facebook or Flickr? Uploading to these sites is virtually the same as uploading to Windows Live, except you'll have to log in first. You may also have to perform a few "authorization" tasks, but once it's set up, it's a breeze to upload photos to your favorite website. Select the photos you want to share, then click:

☐ **Publish > More Services** to publish on Flickr, or to add plug-ins for other social networking websites, like Facebook, YouTube, and Multiply.

Did you know you can create a panoramic photo from multiple photos? Maybe you want to create a panoramic photo of several shots you have of the ocean or a skyline.

Select your three or four shots of a skyline and let Photo Gallery "stitch" them together:

☐ **Make > Create panoramic photo** stitches together multiple photos, like several shots you took of the beach or mountains, to create a single, panoramic photo.

Now you can print the panoramic photo and share it, or give it to a friend as a gift.

Next, try posting an image or images to your blog (you did set up a blog in chapter 2, didn't you?)

☐ **Make > Make a blog post** creates a blog post with Windows Live Writer, a Windows Live free application.

Make a link

Publish your photos to share them with the world.

Take a break

It's time to give your brain a break. Take some time away from this book and your computer to focus on something other than photos. Grab a drink, or go for a walk. You could even do a few sit-ups if you felt like it. It doesn't matter what you do, just make sure it's something other than thinking about Windows. Your brain will thank you for it by working on it in the background while you actively *don't* think about it! When you're ready, come back and start with the Review.

Review

Windows Live Photo Gallery is an application in the Windows Live Essentials suite, a free download from Microsoft. It's important to obtain Windows Live Photo Gallery because Windows 7 does not come with a photo-editing program.

↺ Windows Live Photo Gallery helps you manage the photos you have everywhere including:

a. Old ....

b. .... cards.

c. Digital ....

d. Images from .... pages.

e. Shoeboxes and photo albums (via your scanner).

↺ Windows Live Photo Gallery lets you:

a. Import photos from a .... camera, scanner, ... phone, or .... card.

b. Manage and .... photos in .... and subfolders you create.

c. .... photos by fixing problems with exposure, tint, and sharpness.

d. .... and crop photos.

e. Add black and white ....

↺ Right-clicking any photo in Photo Gallery offers options to:

a. Rotate the image .... or ....

b. Set as .... background.

c. Copy, ... and ....

d. View the photo's .... including size and rating.

↺ Within Photo Gallery you can share photos by:

a. .... them.

b. Saving them to ....

c. Publishing them to a ....

d. Ordering .... online.

e. Playing a ....

Continues, flip the page

○ How would you want create a slideshow for a birthday party or other event?

○ Do you want to create a black and white photo of your family, dressed up in western gear? How would you do that?

○ What could you do with panoramic pictures you've created with images you've taken of a skyline or ocean view?

How did you do?

Did you forget anything? It's hard to remember it all. Go ahead and re-read the sections covering what you overlooked. Your brain might need a bit more time to absorb all the information.

Experiment

The best way to really cement these features and techniques into your long-term memory is to expand on the techniques you learned in the chapter by using them and taking them just one step further.

Here are some suggestions for your experiment using techniques covered in this chapter.

Create a DVD with Live Photo Gallery and Windows DVD Maker

Do you have a relative who doesn't have a computer and/or an Internet connection? Maybe it's your grandmother or grandfather, or a child that's not quite old enough to use a computer yet. How can you share your favorite photos with them, short of printing them and putting them in the mail? That can get expensive.

You can share hundreds of photos (and even videos) by creating a DVD using Windows DVD Maker.

To start, in Windows Live Photo Gallery, click **Make**, and click **Burn a DVD**. Follow the prompts to create a DVD that can be played on almost any DVD player, even the one your Grandma has connected to her TV. You can add titles and credits, music, and even menu text, just like a real DVD!

Now you can share your favorite photos and events with anyone!

Of course, you can also use Windows Live Photo Gallery to play with the other photo Fix options:

1. If auto adjust still leaves an image too dark or too bright, you can **Adjust exposure** and change the brightness, contrast, shadows, and highlights yourself.

2. If your photo came out all red, you can use the **Adjust color** option to change the color temperature (red is hot, blue is cold), tint, and saturation.

3. Photos taken at night typically look grainy, but you can use the **Adjust detail** option to sharpen the photo or reduce noise.

4. **Black and white effects** are kinda fun! Try applying black and white effects to images so the photos look old. Try it on a recent (color) picture of your grandparents or parents.

Tip: Want more editing tools? Click **Extra**, and then click **Download more photo tools**.

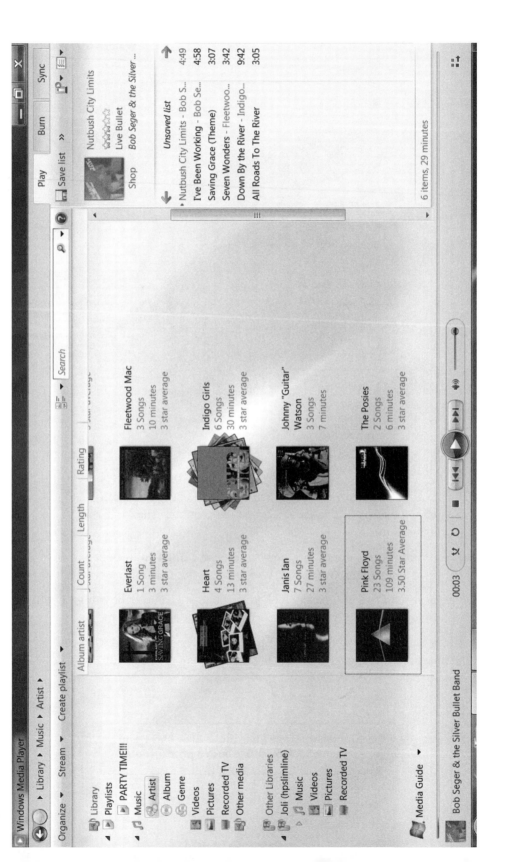

5 Windows Media Player

Do you have music everywhere? On your old PC(s), an MP3 player, or even still on CDs? Maybe you've downloaded music files that you play in iTunes or in Zune. Now you have a new Windows 7 computer and it would be great to get all your music in one place, but how, and will it work the way you want?

⇨ What music can you play on your Windows 7 PC?

⇨ Does the music player play MP3 and MP4 files?

⇨ What about AAC files? And WMA?

⇨ What about music you've purchased from iTunes?

No Problem!

Windows 7 comes with a great program for managing your music. Windows Media Player can help you:

⇨ Access media on other networked PCs without having to move or copy the data to your new one.

⇨ Rip and burn music easily, and play music in new ways with improved playback features.

⇨ Create personalized lists of songs you like for any occasion, and save the list for future use.

⇨ Pick up media information regarding music, movies, TV, games, and Internet radio with its Windows Media Guide.

If you have other Windows 7 PCs on a home network, there's even more reason to commit to Windows Media Player. The **Play to** option allows you to select media on one PC and play it on another. You can also access your media via an Internet connection. This means you can access the media on your desktop PC from your laptop while you're away from home.

Access music on other PCs

Got music? Sure you do; you're not new to the music scene. You've ripped your CD collection and acquired music from various sources on the Web. You've used iTunes or Zune. You've even created CDs for the car. But are you going to have to start over if you want to listen to your music now?

There are three ways to access the music you have on other PCs on your home network. You can:

→ **Copy** or **move** the data to your new PC.

→ **Add the networked PC's music folders** to your Media Player library.

→ **Enable Remote Media Streaming** to allow access to media over the Internet from another Windows 7 PC.

But how do you know which option's right for you?

Do you have a laptop you'd like to copy music to? If you **copy** your music files, and put them on your new PC, laptop or netbook, the music will be on the computer and will always be available (this is great for portable computers). It's also a good approach if you need a place to **back up** your music.

Is your music on a computer you'd like to retire, or one you no longer trust? You could **move** your music files to your new PC and remove them from the old one.

Maybe your music's stored on a PC that's always on and connected to your home network. Will you have to move everything to your Windows 7 PC? You can **add** the music library from a networked PC and access the files from your Windows 7 PC.

The only problem with the latter scenario is that the networked computer holding the data must be turned on and connected to the network for you to access it.

Do you want access to your media from anywhere in the world without having to fill up your laptop's hard drive? If you enable **Remote Media Streaming**, you can access the files in that computer's music library from anywhere in the world.

Now you've seen the benefits of copying, moving, adding libraries, and enabling remote access here, which will you use? If you have multiple computers, will you use the same approach with each of them? Let's take a look at all the ways you can access music so you can decide for yourself.

Copy and move, and into the groove

Do you want to **copy** music to a laptop *and* **move** it off an ailing PC? You already know how to copy and move data, so you can do this real quick. This is the option to use if you want to retire an older computer or give it to your kids, turn it off and leave it off, or if it's just about ready for the computer graveyard. It's also a good idea if you want your new Windows 7 PC to run all your media. There are quite a few advantages to this, as you'll see later in this chapter.

The Windows 7 Media Player looks to your **Music Library** for music files. So, if you're going to move or copy data to your Windows 7 PC, the Music Library is where it'll need to go:

1. Click **Start > Music**. This brings up the Music Library. Use Snap to position this window on the left-hand side of the screen.

2. Click **Start** again, then **Documents**. In the new window, browse to the older machine on the network where the music files you'd like to move are located. Snap this window to the right of your screen.

3. In the older machine's window, click **Organize** then click **Select all**.

4. Right-click the files and drag them to the Music Library in the left pane.

5. Drop the files into the Music Library, and click **Move**.

What happens to the music files in both libraries?

> Do you want to copy files instead of moving them? When you drop the files in Step 5, click Copy.

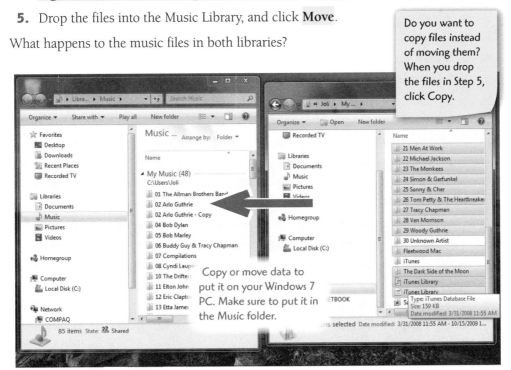

Copy or move data to put it on your Windows 7 PC. Make sure to put it in the Music folder.

Access music files over a network

What if your music's already on another trusted PC that's always available? Do you have to move everything to your Windows 7 PC? You can access all the media on the other machine over the network. You don't have to move or copy the data. This may be the best option if you're configuring a computer in a family or media room with the intention of accessing shared media from it. Can you see any downsides to this option?

First, you have to make sure that the PC that already holds the music you want to share has media sharing enabled. In Windows Media Player 12 you configure that from the **Stream** menu. In older versions of Media Player, you'll have to look around for it. Try the Library tab, and look for Media Sharing for starters. If you can't find it, you can always look under Tools and Options.

In Media Player 12, you want to enable **Automatically allow devices to play my media**. Also select **Allow remote control of my player**. Then opt to allow all computers and devices when prompted.

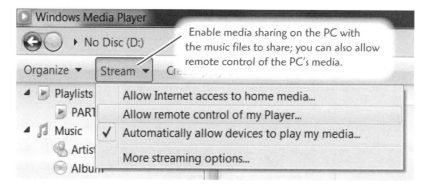

Enable media sharing on the PC with the music files to share; you can also allow remote control of the PC's media.

Now, on your Windows 7 PC:

1. Go to Media Player and click the arrow next to **Organize**.

2. Click **Manage Libraries > Music**.

Media Player offers an easy way to add media from another computer's Music Library.

3. Click **Add**, and browse to the location of the networked library. Find the folder in the next dialog and click **Include folder**.

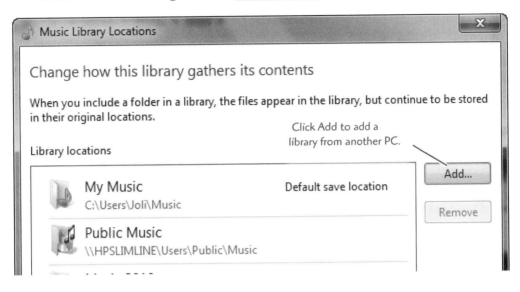

4. Click OK.

5. Go ahead and enable media sharing on this PC too. Click **Stream**, and click **Automatically allow devices to play my media**.

6. For good measure, click **Organize > Apply Media Changes** to make Media Player look for updated file information and apply the updates immediately.

Warning
You can't access shared media on a PC that's turned off or not connected to the network!

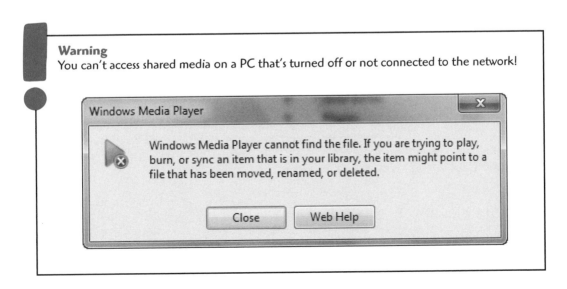

Play with it

Spend a little time now playing a few tracks of the music you copied, moved, added, or can now access over the network. Although it's new, this version of Media Player should look familiar. Simply find the song or album you want to play and click it.

As with other versions of Media Player, there are controls at the bottom of the window and a button for switching to Now Playing view. From there you can select Full Screen mode, go back to the Library, and more.

Access your media from anywhere

Have you ever found yourself at a friend or relative's house, been on vacation, or been in a meeting and wished you could access the media on your home PC? Before now, that was nearly impossible, at least for most of us. With Windows 7 you can set up **Remote Media Streaming** at home, and access your media over the Internet from anywhere on your Windows 7 PC.

Accessing media remotely is ideal if you travel with a small computer like a netbook, and you simply don't have space for all your media on it. It's also a neat way to share videos from home: your family can load videos at their convenience, and you can view the videos whenever it suits you. No e-mailing, no muss, no fuss!

The only downside to this option is that you'll need two Windows 7 computers. One at home that's connected to the Internet, set up to share media, and is always on (even sleeping is out for this machine). The other computer needs access to the first computer via the Internet. This is a good option if you travel frequently.

Start with the machine that holds the files you want to access remotely. *It needs to be running Windows 7:*

1. In Windows Media Player 12 click **Stream**, and click **Allow Internet access to home media**.

2. Click **Link an online ID** and choose your online ID (it could be your Windows Live ID or an ID from another provider). Click OK to complete the link process.

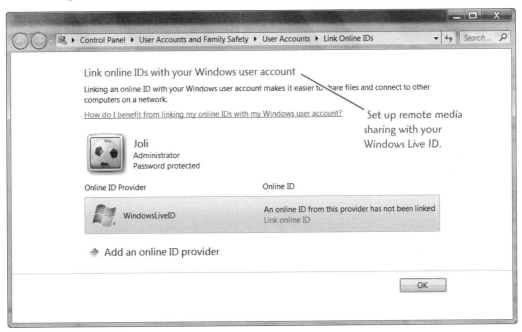

3. Click **Allow access to home media**.

Repeat these steps on the netbook, laptop, or a PC away from home that you'll use to access the media. This also needs to be running Windows 7. Look under Other Libraries for the PC that holds the media. Do you see it? Provided the computer that's streaming the files is turned on and connected to the Internet, you'll see all it listed under Other Libraries and be able to access the files it holds.

Play with it

Do you have a Digital Living Network Alliance (DLNA) compliant device connected to your network? If you do and you've created a HomeGroup (see chapter 13) and enabled media sharing on your Windows 7 PC, you can access one more feature of Windows Media Player: **Play To**.

This new feature in Windows 7 allows you to select media on one PC and play it on another device (including another Windows 7 PC). But you have to jump through a few hoops first.

After you've purchased and set up a compatible player, connected it to the network, turned it on, created a HomeGroup, and enabled media sharing—phew!—simply right-click any media (a song, album, picture, video, or anything similar), and select **Play To**.

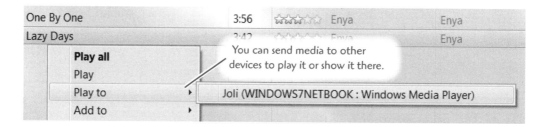

Make sure the device you want to send the file to and play it on is turned on, connected to the network and ready to accept music. And if you're sending the music to another Windows 7 PC, make sure Windows Media Player is open on that PC.

New ways to play music

Windows 7 has introduced some cool new features that you can access not from Media Player, but from the Taskbar.

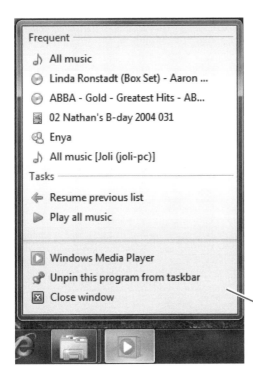

Use a Jump List to access your music

Have you ever wanted a quick way to see music you've recently played, all music, and media you frequently view? Windows 7 has introduced new ways to access your music: **Jump Lists**. To access a **Jump List**, right-click the Media Player icon in the Taskbar.

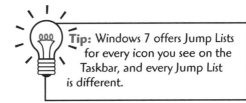

Tip: Windows 7 offers Jump Lists for every icon you see on the Taskbar, and every Jump List is different.

Jump Lists are a feature of Windows 7 that also works well with Media Player. Right-click the Media Player icon to access its jump list.

New playback modes

Wouldn't it be great if you could minimize Windows Media Player to the Taskbar, and still be able to play or pause music without opening the program? You're in luck; you can. Your computer has to support it though, and while most do, if your computer is old or doesn't have the required resources, you may be one of the unlucky few who can't use this feature. If you aren't sure, test it! Just hover the cursor over the icon in the Taskbar to access these playback options.

Can't remember if you like a song or not or if it's the song you're looking for? Hover the mouse over the song title and click Preview to hear a 15-second song preview.

Make a link

Hover the cursor over the icons in the Taskbar or right-click them to access new functions in Windows 7.

Sync an MP3 player

Connect your MP3 player and see what happens. If you have an MP3 device you want to add music to, or if the device already contains music, connect it and see what happens.

Did you plug in your iPod? Did Windows Media Player recognize it? Did Media Player play nice with your Zune? Sadly you can't sync a Zune (even though it's made by Microsoft), iPhone, or iPod with Windows Media Player because those all require special software (like iTunes). So if none of these work, does *anything* sync with Media Player?

You *can* sync a generic portable MP3 player and you may find synchronizing with Media Player could be a better option than the software the player came with.

If your player was recognized when you plugged it in, that means it's compatible with Media Player and you'll see options to automatically sync or drag items to the device manually, depending on the size of the player.

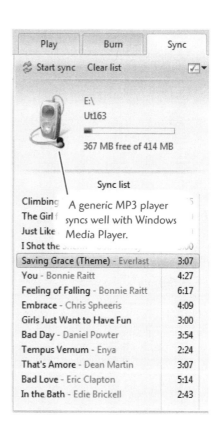

Is the device is over 4 GB? Or will your entire library fit on it? If so, you can opt for **Automatic Sync**. With this option, your entire music library is synced automatically each time you connect the device. You don't need to move or copy anything. Media Player will update your player automatically when you plug it in.

If your device is less than 4GB, your entire library won't fit on it, or you want to manually configure the device with specific playlists and songs, you can opt for the **Manual Sync** option. If you opt for manual sync, you'll need to drag songs or albums to the Sync pane until you run out of music or space.

How much control do you have over what's synced in either Sync option?

Play with it

You can set higher priorities for your favorite playlists if you can't fit all of your music on the device, and you can switch from automatic to manual any time. You can even opt for Shuffle what syncs, if desired. Don't forget to click Start Sync when you're ready.

Do Burn, Rip, Visualizations, Pictures, Videos, and Playlists still work the same way?

Now that you're in the know about all the new stuff, where's the old stuff? It's all there, in pretty much the same places. Did you notice the **Play** and **Burn** tabs to the right of Sync? Click the tabs to play and burn. Simple enough.

Try inserting a CD. What happens? Yup, the **Rip** command appears. There's easy access to **Create Playlist**, too, and you can click the arrow beside it to create an auto playlist.

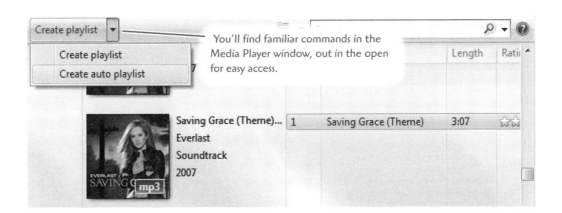

You'll find familiar commands in the Media Player window, out in the open for easy access.

Can you still change the look of your Media Player? Press Alt on your keyboard to access the View menu.

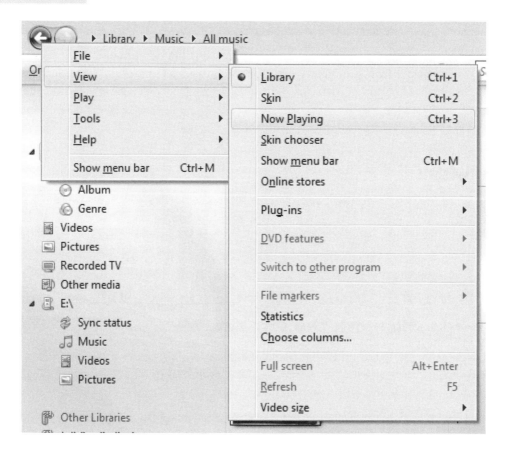

From there you can show the Menu bar, access online stores, switch to Now Playing view, and choose new skins. Here's the skin "Toothy", available for download.

You can give Media Player new skins via the View menu. You can even download new skins.

But where did the visualizations go? Well that's a little trickier. Here's how to get to those:

1. Play any song or playlist.

2. Switch to **Now Playing** using the icon in the bottom right corner or from the View menu.

3. Right-click inside the Now Playing window and click **Visualizations**.

4. Select one.

What other options do you see in the Now Playing window? There are enhancements here too, like options to show lyrics, captions, and subtitles.

Finally, go back to the Music library and click the arrow next to Library. What do you see? Browse through the options, click Videos, Pictures, Recorded TV, Other media, or Playlists. We'll come back to watching TV in chapter 7.

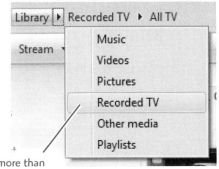

Windows Media Player does more than play music; it can also handle videos, pictures, recorded TV, and more.

- -

Take a break

It's that time again. Lucky you. It's time to take a break. You may be tempted to keep forging ahead, but fight the urge. Studies show that your retention of new material will actually increase if you walk away now and then to give your learning muscles a much deserved break. So, go take a break, if for no other reason than that the science made you do it.

Review

Things to remember:

↻ You can .... CDs you own or .... CDs of music you've paid for.

↻ Jump Lists let you .... from the ....

↻ Hover your cursor over the Media Player icon in the Taskbar to
....

↻ Press the .... key to access the View menu.

↻ You can access visualizations two ways:

1. Switch to .... using the icon in the bottom right
corner.

2. From the .... menu.

There are many ways to manage, share, and/or consolidate the music you already have. You can:

↻ .... or .... music from one PC to another.

↻ Add networked PCs' music .... to your Windows 7 Media Player
.... to access the music in them.

↻ Share your Windows 7 .... with other computers on your network.

↻ Enable .... to allow access to media over the
Internet from another Windows 7 PC.

↻ Play music stored on a Windows 7 PC on a compatible device with
....

↻ Create .... for specific occasions or moods.

↻ .... music with an MP3 player.

How did you do?

Did you forget anything? It's hard to remember it all. Go ahead and re-read the sections covering anything you may have overlooked. Your brain might need a bit more time to absorb all the information.

Experiment

Use some of the techniques you just read about. Here are a few ideas to get you started. You can accomplish these experiments with the knowledge you've gained in this chapter and earlier chapters.

Create a playlist

In the Windows Media Player window click Create Playlist. Creating a playlist is the same as it ever was, just name it and drag songs to it. Then you can play the songs in the list, burn them to a CD, or sync them with a music player, among other things.

Think about the reasons you play music. Is it an after-bar get-together? Do you listen to music to fall asleep? Do you put on music when you have guests? Create a playlist for each instance. When you're ready, just put on the playlist that suits your mood.

video library

play all

folders >   date taken   shared

Sample Videos

Las Vegas Strip

Nikko and the Plastic Ba...

Speex_demo

Las Vegas Strip
3/14/2009 0:00:25

6 Windows Media Player vs Windows Media Center

It was easy enough to organize your music in the last chapter, but the problem is that there seem to be *two* programs for working with media in Windows 7. How do you decide which program to use for the media you want to view, watch, or listen to?

⇨ Should you watch recorded TV in Media Player or Media Center?

⇨ Which program is better for managing and playing music?

⇨ What's the best way to view movies on DVDs or personal footage you've recorded with a digital camera?

No Problem!

Windows 7 comes with built-in libraries for storing media, so you don't need to worry about where to store and organize media files. But viewing your media is a different story:

⇨ You can watch recorded TV in Media Player or Media Center.

⇨ You can view pictures and watch home videos in Media Center, Media Player, or even Windows Live Photo Gallery.

⇨ You can listen to music in Media Center, Media Player, and myriad third-party programs, like iTunes.

Sometimes a program seems to be better suited to a task and sometimes it's down to preference, so let's dive in and work out what's best for you.

Get organized

You copied, moved, and shared the music you have on various computers and devices in chapter 5. The problem is that you didn't do that with other media, and you need to. Before moving forward, you should complete the steps necessary and consolidate your pictures, videos, home movies, and recorded TV, as well as any other data that's important to you. Refer to chapter 5 for guidelines such as these:

→ For media on an *older PC* you plan to retire soon, sell, or hand down, *move* all of your media off of it, or **back it up** to your Windows 7 PC.

→ For media on *SD media cards*, **copy** or **move** the data to your Windows 7 PC.

→ For *video and pictures* stored on a trustworthy PC, **share the folder** or **move the data to Public folders** for easy access over a network. (Sharing is discussed in chapters 11 and 12.)

> The steps to copy or move files are just the same as they were for your music files, regardless of the kind of media files you're working with.

Once you have your data copied, moved, backed up, shared, made public, or otherwise available, start by configuring Media Player to access the media in those libraries.

In **Media Player**, click **File > Manage Libraries**. From there, you can select an option (Video, Pictures, and Recorded TV), and work through the process to add any network folders not currently included.

Once you've added media folders and shared folders, you can access them using Media Player's Navigation pane.

You can now access any shared media in Media Player, even recorded TV from other computers. Just like with your music files, click the media to view or play it.

Watch a video

So you want to watch a video you've shot with your own digital video camera or videos you've obtained from the Internet. You could use Windows Media Player or Windows Media Center, but which is better for viewing video? Or is it just a matter of preference?

Because you already know how to use Windows Media Player, open it, click **Videos**, and double-click "Wildlife in HD" to view this video. Where does the video open?

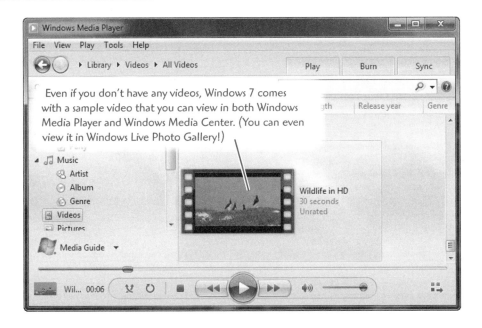

Do you see the familiar controls to stop, pause, rewind, fast-forward, and change the volume in the new video window? (Click Go to Library when the video ends.)

If you're used to Media Player you already understand how to navigate through the folders, access music, pictures, and videos, and you can burn, rip, and sync music. So, that's all fine.

But what if you want to watch TV on your computer? Does it look like Media Player gives you the option to watch *live* TV? How about *recorded* TV? What about creating TV *recordings*? And do you see anything about *Internet TV*?

Media Center

Since there's a lot of other media available online and you can't open all of it in Media Player, wouldn't it be great if you could access all of that too without having to open a separate program to access your music? Windows 7 comes with a program that lets you do all of those things and more: **Media Center**.

Open **Media Center**. It's not on the Taskbar like Media Player, but it is on the Start menu, in All Programs. If you're prompted to set it up, choose **Express**.

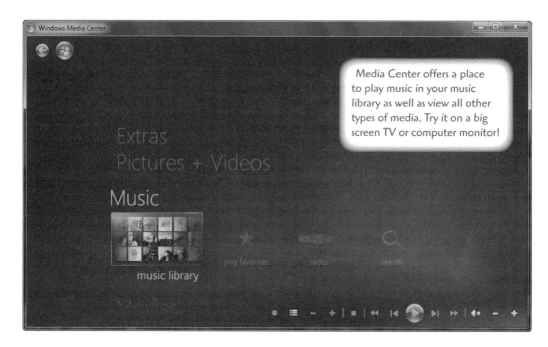

Once Media Center's open, go to Music and click Music Library. What happens?

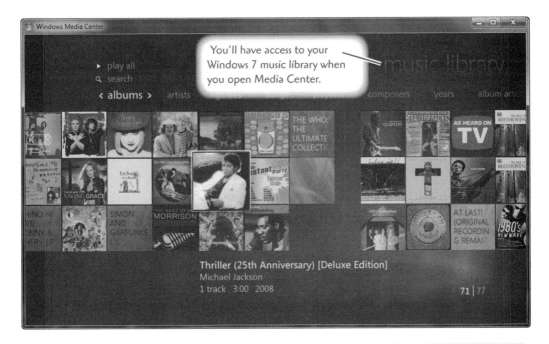

Just like in Media Player you have access to your music, but Media Center lets you access your pictures, videos, and TV, too.

Play with it

Remember the "Wildlife in HD" sample video you played in Media Player? Let's play it in Media Center so you can compare the two applications to see which one you like better, for videos at least.

Use the arrow keys on your keyboard, the mouse, or a Windows Media Center-compatible remote control to access the video library. Open the library, double-click **Sample Videos**, and play "Wildlife in HD".

Move your cursor over the bottom part of the screen. What happens? Try rewind, fast-forward, pause, and stop.

What are the differences between Media Player and Media Center so far? What's the same? Do you like one program over the other yet?

View pictures, view a sample TV recording, and explore extras

Play around with Media Center some more. Browse to and play the following media, included with Windows 7:

→ TV > recorded tv > Landscapes

→ Pictures + Videos > picture library > play slide show

→ Movies > play DVD

Configure Media Center's Media Libraries

Do you remember how you told Media Player where it should look for media earlier in this chapter? You added folders from either the same computer or a networked one in the Navigation pane for Media Player to "watch" and access media from. You need to tell Media Center where your media is, so you can access it. How do you think you'll configure Media Center's Libraries?

Click **Tasks > Settings > Media Libraries**. Now, select a media library to configure, and work through the steps to add it.

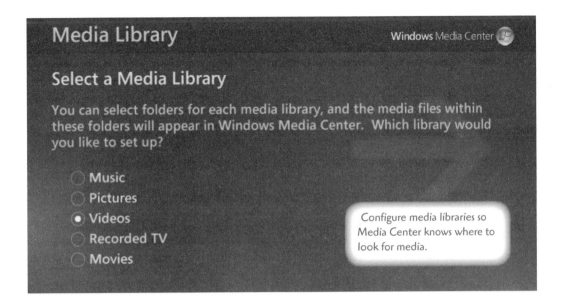

Adding folders to the library is as easy as it was in Media Player. Add folders that contain media that's relevant on this computer or another on the network to the library, then verify you want to use the locations selected. Repeat these steps for other media you want to access. Where does the media appear once you've added it?

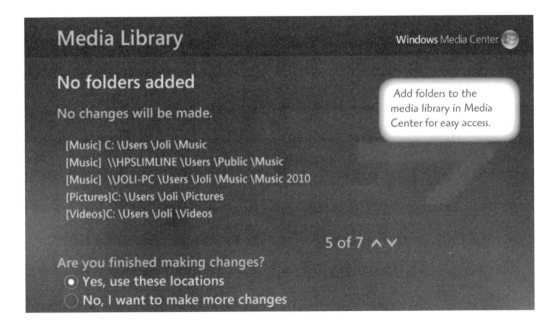

Once libraries are set up, it's easy to access and play media like you do in any other program; select the media to play.

While you've been exploring Media Center, have you noticed anything about how your media has been categorized? Take a look at the music library. What do you see?

The music library has options across the top of the screen including albums, artists, genres, songs, playlists, composers, years, album artists, and shared.

What happens if you choose album view?

So what's new in Media Center?

So what's new? What can you do now that you couldn't do in Windows Vista's version of Media Center or Windows XP's?

Windows Media Center will now play **new types of media**. Do you have any HD TV or digital programs? Media Center will play those. It will also play other file types you may be familiar with, including AAC, MPEG-4, WMV, and WMA. Media Center also supports most AVI, DivX, MOV, and Xvid files, so you can really play just about everything.

Did you ever want to just zip through listings to find what you wanted real quick? Media Center gives you **Turbo Scroll**. Browse the Guide and press the left or right arrow keys for a few seconds. What happens? Do you see the day and approximate time appear across the top of the listings?

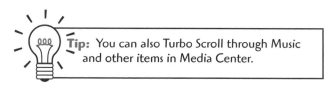

Tip: You can also Turbo Scroll through Music and other items in Media Center.

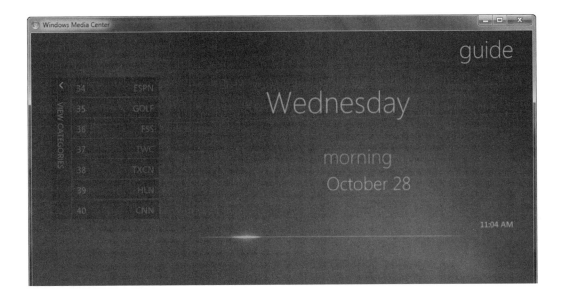

The **Photo Wall** feature offers a new way to share the Media Center experience with others, during music playback. But how do you make the wall appear? You don't have to do anything, just play a song and the album covers will fill the screen. If you want to use your own pictures, click **Play Pictures**.

By default the album covers will fill the screen. If you want to use your own pictures, click Play Pictures.

If you like the Photo Wall, why not find the **Slide Show Maker** in Pictures + Videos and create a slide show from your favorite music or picture library? Just name the slide show then select the images to add to it. After selecting images from one folder you have the option to add images from another, until you've selected all of the images you want to include. The slide show will appear in your Picture library in Media Center. Interestingly, it will also appear in Media Player as a playlist.

Make a link

What do you put in a slide show? Pictures + Videos, that's what!

There's a new **Media Center Desktop Gadget**, too. Find it in the Desktop Gadget Gallery and play with it. What does the Media Center Desktop Gadget let you do?

With the Media Center gadget you can have quick access to recorded TV, sports, movies, and other Media Center data. You'll even see information pulled from the Guide.

And of course, you can add **media extenders**. A **media extender** allows you to pull media from a network PC and play it on the extender on another device in your home. One of the most popular extenders is the Xbox 360. The option to add an extender is located under Tasks.

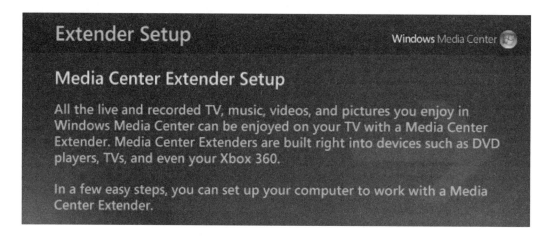

Extender Setup   Windows Media Center

Media Center Extender Setup

All the live and recorded TV, music, videos, and pictures you enjoy in Windows Media Center can be enjoyed on your TV with a Media Center Extender. Media Center Extenders are built right into devices such as DVD players, TVs, and even your Xbox 360.

In a few easy steps, you can set up your computer to work with a Media Center Extender.

Media Player or Media Center, which is better?

What if you've used Media Player and Media Center, and you like them both? How do you know which to use, and for what? Can you decide between the two, or is it just a case of personal preference? Is one better at playing music, and one better for TV for instance?

Both Media Player and Media Center play DVDs, music, and videos, both let you create playlists, burn CDs, view slideshows of pictures, and access media on other PCs on your network, and both play TV shows you've recorded.

	Task	Media Player	Media Center	Notes
Listen	Listen to music	*	*	Media Player is the more popular of the two for managing and listening to music. It seems to take fewer clicks to get to the music you want, and it's got the Burn and Play tabs built right in. It's really easy to create playlists with drag and drop and it's equally easy to burn a playlist to a CD.
	Manage music	*	*	
	Create playlists	*	*	
	Burn and rip CDs	*	*	
	Sync music players	*		
	View/change visualizations	*	*	
	Stream media over your home network	*	*	Both programs let you to stream media to your home network and allow remote control of the player, but if you want to configure Internet access to home media from another PC running Media Center, you'll need to use Media Player.
	Configure Internet access to home media	*		
	Control player remotely	*	*	

Task	Media Player	Media Center	Notes
Watch video	*	*	Media Center and Media Player can both play all types of videos. Here, the two are side by side. Once videos start to play, the controls are virtually the same. For videos, it's simply a matter of preference.
Default player for DVDs	*		DVDs play by default in Media Player and some movies do appear to play better in Media Player. If a movie won't play in Media Center, try the Media Player instead.
Watch DVDs	*	*	Media Center offers more perks, though: you can configure remote control options if you have one, turn on subtitles, and apply audio settings right inside the interface. You even have access to Dolby decoder settings.

Watch Video & DVDs

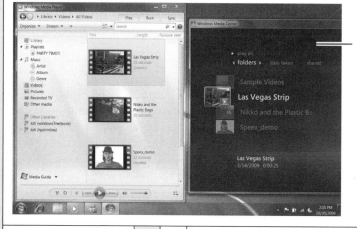

A side-by-side comparison of Media Player and Media Center shows the stark differences in their interfaces.

	Task	Media Player	Media Center	Notes
Watch TV	Watch recorded TV	*	*	For TV, Media Center wins hands down. You can't watch or record live TV in Media Player, though you can watch recorded TV there. Media Center is where you'll spend all your TV time. You'll learn all about TV in the next chapter.
	Watch Live TV		*	
	Record Live TV		*	
	Access Netflix and Internet TV		*	If you're into sports, and want the option to follow fantasy sports leagues, or manage your media subscriptions (like Netflix).
New Features	AAC, MPEG-4, WMV, and WMA file support	*	*	Media Center also supports most AVI, DivX, MOV, and Xvid files
	Turbo Scroll		*	Browse the Guide, faster!
	Photo Wall		*	Displays album covers or your own pictures.
	Slide Show Maker		*	Create a slide show from video and pictures.
	Desktop Gadget	*		
	Media Extenders		*	The most popular extender is the Xbox 360.

So apart from watching live or Internet TV, the choice between the two boils down to a matter of preference. To help you decide, use both programs when you do your various media-related tasks, and see what program you like best for which type of media.

- -

Take a break

Phew! That was a vault of information. Give your brain a break. Go do something else for a while. Got a magazine to read? Need to check your email? Do that now and we'll see you back here in 10, rested and ready to review, and then dive in and experiment to cement these new skills in your brain.

Review

Use this space to write down what you remember about consolidating more of your media, including videos and pictures, and watching media in both Media Player and Media Center.

↺ Windows Media Player can/cannot play music.

↺ Windows Media Center can/cannot play music.

↺ I prefer Media Player/Media Center for listening to music because

....

↺ I prefer Media Player/Media Center for watching DVDs because

....

↺ Windows Media Player is the .... player for DVDs.

↺ Windows Media Center can/cannot play DVDs.

↺ Media Player, Media Center, and Windows Live Photo Gallery can all play slideshows. True/False. I prefer Media Player/Media Center/ Windows Live Photo Gallery for watching DVDs because

....

↺ I can watch home movies in .... and ....
I prefer .... because ....

↺ I have/haven't got a media extender and I want to add a media extender because ....

↺ Things you *can* do in Media Center that you *cannot* do in Media Player include:

→ .... live TV.

→ Recording ....

→ Pausing, ... , and .... live TV.

→ Watching .... TV.

→ Watching sports on ....

→ Creating .... slide shows.

→ Setting options for a Media Center .... control.

How did you do?

Did you forget anything? It's hard to remember it all. Go ahead and re-read the sections covering what you overlooked. Your brain might need a bit more time to absorb all the information.

Experiment

Use some of the techniques you just read about. Here's an idea to get you started. You can accomplish this experiments with the knowledge you've gained in this and earlier chapters.

Media extender support is built into Windows Media Center

If you've been thinking about getting a media extender, already have an Xbox 360, or would like to learn more about extenders, click **Tasks > add extender**. A wizard will walk you through the process.

7 Watch TV on your computer

You've heard that you can watch TV on your computer and you know that would really help for one or several of the following reasons:

⇨ You *don't* have a digital video recorder (DVR) but you want to be able to record your favorite TV shows.

⇨ You *do* have a DVR, but there's not enough space on it to record everything you want to watch.

⇨ You want to cut the cost of renting a DVR from your cable TV provider.

⇨ You want to watch recorded TV on your laptop in a hotel room or on a netbook while waiting for a plane at the airport.

⇨ You want to explore Internet TV.

But how do you know if your computer is set up so you can watch TV? Or if you need to get it set up, is it complicated to do?

No Problem!

You've already met Media Center, and with the proper hardware you can record your favorite live TV shows and save them to your computer's hard drive.

⇨ Once the TV shows are on your hard drive you can watch the recorded shows anywhere you can take your computer.

⇨ You can use Windows Media Center's recording features instead of your cable company's DVR and DVR service.

⇨ You can share the media on your computer with other computers and compliant media devices on your network. This means you can record TV on your home office PC, and share that media to an Xbox 360, compatible media extender, other Windows 7 PCs, or other devices.

Is your computer TV-ready?

Before you go any further you need to find out if you can watch and record television on your PC. You can only watch live TV on your computer if it has a TV tuner and you've configured the tuner to work with your TV signal. You'll also need a connection to the Internet and a way to connect to the TV signal (an antenna, cable modem, and so on).

To find out if you have the proper hardware:

1. Open **Media Center**.

2. Use the arrow keys on your keyboard to locate **TV** in the options, and move right through the TV menu until you reach **live tv setup**.

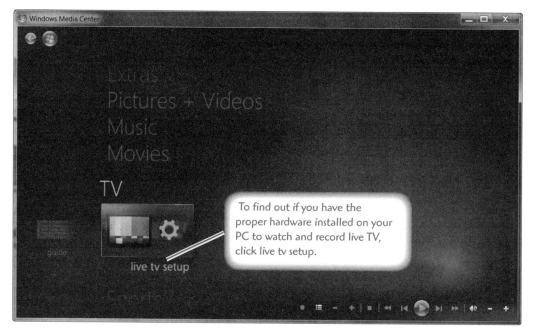

To find out if you have the proper hardware installed on your PC to watch and record live TV, click live tv setup.

3. If you see the option to configure the TV tuner to work with your TV connection, you're ready to work through the configuration process. If you see that no tuner was found, you'll have to buy and install a TV tuner or install a tuner if you already have one.

If you see this, you'll have to visit to the local computer store and purchase a TV tuner.

Tip: Buy and install a TV tuner

What's the most important feature to look for when you're shopping for a TV tuner? First, Windows 7 compatibility. Second, make sure you check it's an actual TV *tuner*, not some kind of antenna. Of course, it's OK to purchase an external TV tuner if you aren't comfortable with installing an internal one (or paying someone else to).

Once the tuner's installed, as long as your computer's turned on and connected to the tuner when the show needs to record, you'll do fine. The TV tuner doesn't need to be connected when you watch a recorded show, so an external tuner will do just fine for a laptop or netbook, and you'll be able to take your recorded shows with you when you travel.

Follow the directions carefully when you install the tuner. Tuners are a lot less finicky than they used to be, but make sure you follow the directions to ensure the install process is successful.

Set up a TV tuner

If your PC came with a built-in TV tuner, or, if you've successfully installed one of your own, open Media Center, scroll to TV > live tv setup. Click the **Setup now** option to get started.

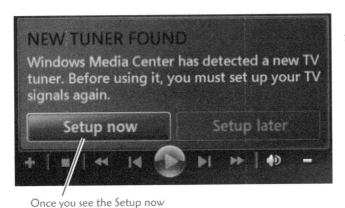

Once you see the Setup now button, you're good to go.

There are a few things you'll need to input or confirm:

→ Your region — That's your country.
→ Your zip code
→ Your TV signal type
→ Your TV signal provider, if applicable

When you're done click **TV**, and **live tv** to check that the signal and tuner are configured correctly. You're watching TV on your PC!

Play with it

Do you detest sitting through commercials? Wouldn't it be nice if you could simply fast-forward through them? But you can't fast-forward live TV. So what's the trick?

While you can't fast-forward through live TV, you can fast-forward through a live TV program you've paused for a bit (this also works with recordings, obviously). Let's say you want to watch a 30-minute show, but you know there's 10 minutes of commercials.

All you have to do is **pause** the show for 10 or 15 minutes, then play it. Any time there's a commercial, you can hit the fast-forward button.

Just pause live TV or start a recorded show and fast-forward through the commercial breaks.

But just where are those pause and fast-forward buttons? Just like when you're watching a DVD, the controls appear when your cursor's over the bottom right part of the screen. Or you could get a Media Center-compatible remote control.

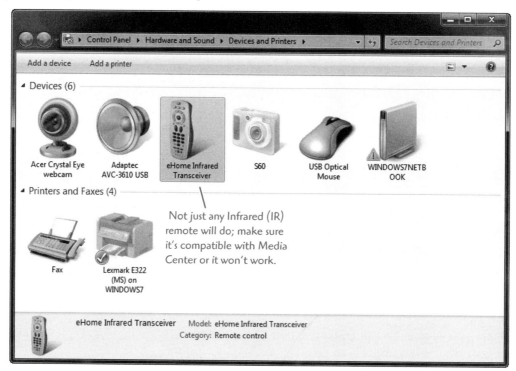

Not just any Infrared (IR) remote will do; make sure it's compatible with Media Center or it won't work.

Improve the picture

Does your computer's TV picture look as good as your actual TV? If you're not happy with the way live TV appears on your TV or monitor, click **Tasks**, then **settings** to configure the display manually.

In the **settings** window there are several options, including one for TV. Click it and once you're in the TV area click **Configure Your TV or Monitor**.

Let Media Center adjust the settings for you in the Display Configuration wizard, and afterwards you can adjust the display settings manually to make Media Center look its best. During the process you'll:

- [ ] Switch to full-screen mode if you aren't in that mode already.
- [ ] Choose a display if more than one display is available.
- [ ] Choose the type of display you use.

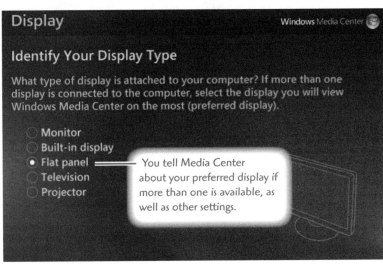

- [ ] Configure the width of the display (4:3 or 16:9).
- [ ] Confirm your display resolution.

Once you've confirmed your choices, you may need to work through specific configuration tasks related to your hardware depending on what you opt for in the display wizard and the kind of hardware you have. You may also be prompted to configure things like display calibration, aspect ratio, contrast, and other options.

Record some TV!

Are there TV sitcoms you want to see, movies you want to watch, and reality TV shows you need to catch up on? Do you have the time to watch these when they're on? What if you'd like to see the evening news every night, but you're not home at 5:30 p.m. to watch it then? And, since you're the only one who likes Longhorn Sports Center Weekly, would you like to record that to watch later too? You can do all of this and more with Media Center's record feature.

What's the easiest way to record TV in Media Center? If you're watching something and you decide you want to record the rest of it to watch later, bring up the controls on the Media Center screen and if that show's available to record, you'll see the red **Record** button. Try it now, bring up the Guide and select a show. What happens to the controls?

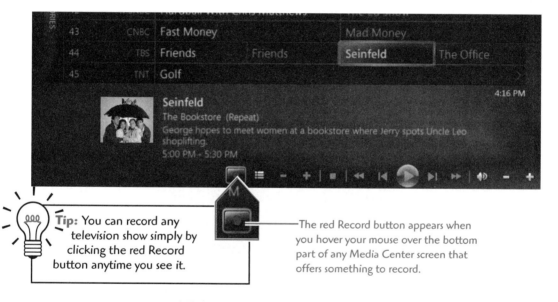

Tip: You can record any television show simply by clicking the red Record button anytime you see it.

The red Record button appears when you hover your mouse over the bottom part of any Media Center screen that offers something to record.

Beyond clicking the Record button, what else can you do with the Guide? Use the arrow keys to move through the Guide, look for programs using Categories, and more.

But if it's got everything, how will you find your shows? Can you filter the Guide to find just the shows you like?

Almost everything you're looking for is in the Guide.

With the Guide open, click the arrow next to **View Categories** to show the category options shown here. Click Search and type keywords or the title of the show you're looking for.

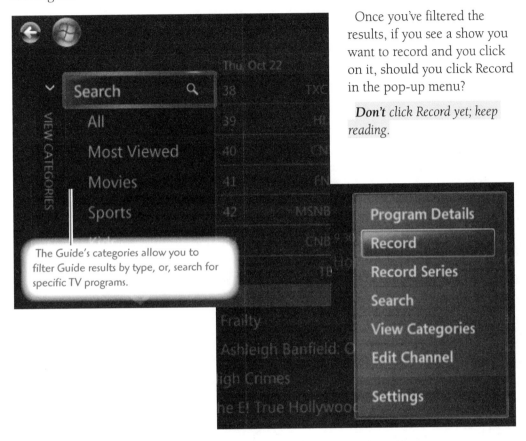

The Guide's categories allow you to filter Guide results by type, or, search for specific TV programs.

Once you've filtered the results, if you see a show you want to record and you click on it, should you click Record in the pop-up menu?

Don't click Record yet; keep reading.

So, should you choose Record from the Guide? If you do, by default Media Center creates a series recording and will now record the *entire series*, **including reruns**. And if you recorded all your favorite shows this way, you'd fill up your hard drive in a matter of weeks because Media Center will record *all* instances of shows, including reruns.

So, is there any way to record just one show from any season?

Tip: To record a single episode of a show without creating a series recording, **right-click the show *then click Record***. Try it now, select a couple of shows that are on right now and record them. You'll need them in a moment.

Is it really possible to fill up your computer's hard drive in only a few weeks?

Would recording a few of your favorite series really fill up your 200 GB hard drive in only a few weeks? Yes, it would. There are several reasons why, but there are steps you can take to avoid this almost inevitable (and built-in) problem with Media Center.

On the Media Center home screen, click Tasks, click settings, click TV > **Recorder**. Here's where you can see how many hours you can use for recorded TV.

In the screenshot below, some TV has already been recorded, but only about 3 hours' worth. How many hours of TV can Media Center record? How big is the space allocated to hold the recordings?

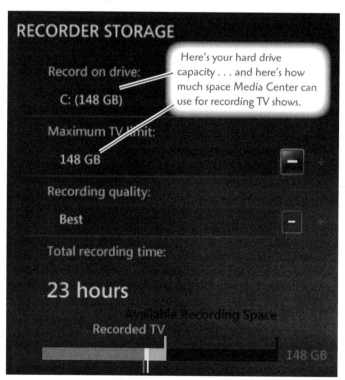

Yikes! The default recording space is *your entire hard drive*. Can you see the problem with that?

You need to find a balance between keeping the most recordings possible while still maintaining a fully functioning computer with ample, free hard drive space. One option is to configure the recording defaults to record TV to an external or network drive. Do you have a home network that shares media? This is a good option for you. This option's not so hot if you want your media with you on a laptop.

So is there any way around filling up your hard drive? A much better option is to change the recording defaults. If you want to save TV to your hard drive, how do you think you could change the default record settings so the recordings don't fill up your hard drive without your knowledge?

Tweak the record settings

If you leave Media Center with its default settings your hard drive will get full quickly. So you need to configure the settings to create a workable compromise between quality and quantity, and make sure you don't record reruns of any new series you record.

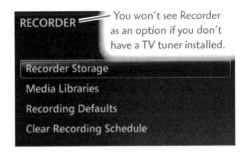

You won't see Recorder as an option *if you don't* have a TV tuner installed.

In Media Center, under Tasks > settings, find **TV**. Click it to see the options up for configuration. Click **Recorder**, and take a look at the **Recorder Storage** and **Recording Defaults**.

Problem	No Problem!	Where to fix it
Your recorded TV shows are deleted or written over before you can watch them.	Record TV on a secondary hard drive.	Recorder > **Recorder Storage**
You ran out of hard drive space.	Reduce the maximum TV limit to half or two-thirds of your hard drive capacity.	Recorder > **Recorder Storage**
After making the previous two adjustments, you still run out of hard drive space or can't record everything you want.	Reduce the quality of the TV you record. Choose Better instead of Best. What happens to the amount of TV you can record?	Recorder > **Recorder Storage**
Some programs you record start early or run late and you're missing integral parts of the show.	Change the recording settings to start and stop a specific amount of time before or after the scheduled airtime.	Recorder > **Recording Defaults**
You've recorded the last two weeks of *David Letterman*, but you really only want to keep two or three episodes at a time.	Change the settings for **Keep up to**. This keeps the most recent episodes only.	Recorder > **Recording Defaults**
You want to keep what you record until you watch it. You don't want anything to be automatically written over or deleted when space is needed for new, scheduled recordings, but once you've watched a recording, you're happy for it to be automatically deleted.	Under Keep, select **Until I watch**. To manually control your recordings, select **Until I delete**.	Recorder > **Recording Defaults**

What other options did you see while working through the table? Did you make any other changes?

Now that you've got one or two shows recorded, in Media Center, locate **TV > recorded tv**. Click any recorded TV program to play it. Click **play** (or **resume**).

While watching, you can:

→ Move your mouse to the bottom of the screen to access controls like rewind, fast forward, pause, volume, and more.

→ Change to full-screen mode by maximizing the Media Center window.

→ Connect external speakers or an external display for better performance.

→ Right-click the screen to show additional information including program info, details, zoom, and captions.

Note: When you click a recording, you'll also see options to delete the show, restart or resume (if you've already started watching it), and scroll through options like actions, other showings, and cast + crew.

Right-click the screen to get more program information.

What does Media Center offer sports fans?

Do you love sports? Do you want to see what's on now, what's on later, who's playing and what the current scores are? Would you like to follow your favorite and fantasy league players? If you have a TV tuner and an Internet connection, you can do all of this and more.

In Media Center, select **Sports**. What do you see? Explore each of the options. Start with **on now**.

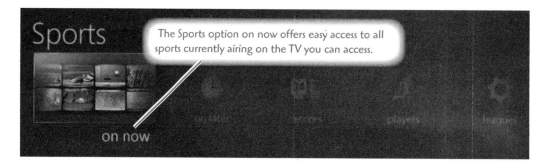

The Sports option on now offers easy access to all sports currently airing on the TV you can access.

Use your mouse or the arrow keys on the keyboard to move among the choices. If you have an Internet connection, do you see the sports news alerts across the bottom of your screen? Now try **on later** to view the sports shows that are on later in the day, and what channel they're on.

Play with it

Track your favorite fantasy league players

In Media Center, under Sports, click **leagues**. Select your sport, select **Track fantasy players**, and click Save. What happens?

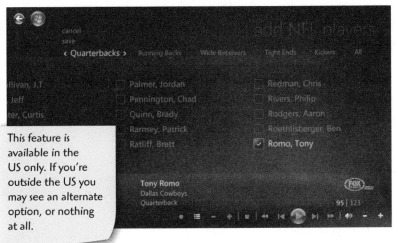

> This feature is available in the US only. If you're outside the US you may see an alternate option, or nothing at all.

Now add the players to follow. Again, under Sports, click **players**, then **add players**. Select the players in your fantasy league, under each category, until you've selected your entire team. Let the fun begin!

Watch Internet TV

If you don't have a TV tuner, or, you've got one but can't take it with you when you travel, can you still watch TV? What if you missed your favorite show last week and didn't record it. Is there any way catch up it now?

Media Center offers **Internet TV** under the TV option. You don't need anything special; just a connection to the Internet. You'll have to perform a few installation tasks, but once you've met those requirements, you can watch Internet TV.

In addition to programming from CBS, NBC, ABC, and the like, some Internet TV offerings are previews, trailers, or sneak peeks, while some offer entire shows. One service, shown here, offers full episodes of Medium, a popular TV show in the U.S..

You can also access Netflix. If you're a member, you can view and watch movies in your Instant Queue; click any movie to play it. If you're not a member, you can review a list of their top rated movies or sign up for membership.

TV channels and services offered vary depending on your location. You may see some, all, or none of these services plus a variety of others if you're outside the US.

Play with it

Open Internet TV and perform any installation tasks. On the Internet TV home screen, use the arrow keys to move through the programs. Click **Watch Now** to see what all the hype is about!

Take a break

Your brain needs time to sift through what you just learned about watching TV in Media Center. Time to take a break. We're nearly at the end of the chapter. All that's left is the Review and Experiment. So walk away and find something else to do for a little while. Now's a great time to read that book sitting on the table next to your bed.

Review

Windows 7's Media Center lets you easily:

↻ .... your favorite TV shows and .... them to your computer's hard drive.

↻ .... the recorded shows anywhere you can take your computer.

↻ .... recorded TV with other .... and compliant media devices on your network.

To watch live TV on Media Center you need:

↻ An internal or external ....

↻ A way to acquire the TV signal, perhaps via antenna, ... , or ....

↻ An .... connection.

Recording defaults in Media Center are not always best:

↻ Series recordings include both .... shows and ....

↻ Shows will continue to record until your .... is completely ....

↻ Shows record at the .... and that uses .... of hard drive space.

↻ Shows record with .... of how many .... of a show to keep.

↻ Shows record to your hard drive, but you can record to .... if you prefer.

When watching live or recorded TV you can:

↻ .... rewind, ... fast forward, ... and perform similar tasks using the .... at the .... of the screen or a compatible ....

↻ Obtain more information about a show by .... its title.

↻ Configure settings by right-clicking any .... in the Recorded TV list.

How did you do?

Did you forget anything? It's hard to remember it all. Go ahead and reread the sections covering what you overlooked. Your brain might need a bit more time to absorb all the information.

Experiment

Experiments like this really help your long-term memory to remember all of these new techniques. Here are some suggestions for your experiment.

Set up a Favorites list

You probably get TV channels you don't watch. Those may include TV channels that broadcast in other languages, home shopping channels, or channels that offer programming you're not interested in, like old movies or cartoons. When channel surfing, you have to browse through those channels even though you're not interested in their content.

Just as you can with your local cable company's DVR or cable box, you can create a Favorites list right inside Media Center. Just name the list and choose what channels you want to include.

To get started, browse to **Tasks > Settings > TV > Guide > Edit Favorites Lineups**.

Connect and configure a second display

If your laptop screen isn't cutting it, add a second display. Almost all laptops offer a port for connecting one, and some desktop PCs do too. It's easy; just connect the display to your laptop and plug it in. Now what? Open Windows 7 Display options. You remember, right? Click Start and type Projector. Click Connect to a projector. You can duplicate what's on your current computer screen, extend your screen over both monitors, or only use the secondary screen.

Once you've got your secondary monitor set up how you like it, repeat the steps for configuring a display in Media Center. You may be able to improve the picture even more!

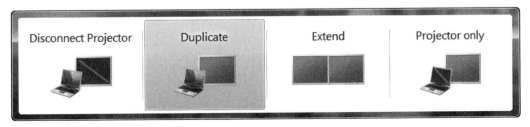

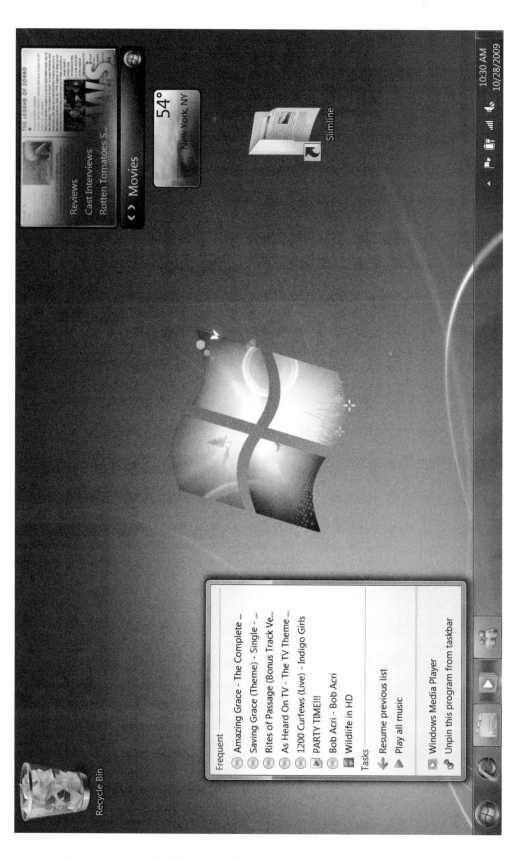

8 Shortcuts and personalization save time

It's amazing how time adds up. Have you ever wondered how much time you spend doing the same common tasks? Things like:

⇨ Locating files and folders.

⇨ Moving among open windows.

⇨ Accessing your favorite programs.

⇨ Having the proper program open when you insert media or connect some hardware.

Those things all take a good few seconds to do and if you do them often enough, those seconds add up to minutes and that's before you add the relentless interruptions from the computer itself to the mix. What you need are timesaving solutions. Fast.

No Problem!

Windows 7 offers lots of ways to do more, faster.

⇨ The Start Search window helps you locate items quickly.

⇨ You can move through windows faster using Flip and Flip 3-D.

⇨ You can use Jump Lists.

⇨ There are improved Taskbar thumbnail views.

⇨ You get the ability to pin programs to the Taskbar and order them the way you like.

⇨ You can even minimize everything to the Desktop with a single click of the mouse.

So what are you waiting for? Let's start saving you some time.

Copy or move your documents

Before we go any further, did you copy or move all your documents over to your Windows 7 PC yet? If you haven't, the steps are just the same as they were for your music, so you can do this real quick.

Windows 7 looks in your **Documents folder** for your documents, just like Vista and XP before it. And as you know now, you can also locate documents in your Documents library. So, if you're going to move or copy your documents to your Windows 7 PC, the Documents folder is where they'll need to go.

Here's one way to move documents from one PC to another:

1. On your old PC, copy the documents you want to move (and that may not be all of the documents you have) to a flash drive.

2. Connect the flash drive to your new Windows 7 PC.

3. Click Start and Computer to access the data on the flash drive if necessary. You can also opt to view the files if prompted by the computer after inserting the device.

4. Select the files to move, and drag them to the Documents folder.

Improved and categorized searches

Have you ever edited a Word document and e-mailed it, and a few weeks later the recipient asks you to resend the file because they lost it? You need to find that e-mail, but how? Have you ever opened a file in an e-mail, worked on it, and clicked Save without stating where on the hard drive to save it? Now the document's stored in some obscure temporary folder that's not in any libraries or folders and you need the information it contains. Now. How will you find it?

Start Search is the answer to all your lost file problems. Type anything you like into the Start Search window to see a short list of pertinent results. Try it. Type the name of your pet, or partner or kiddo into the Start Search field. What happens?

Do the results show what you're looking for, or are the results broader? In our first

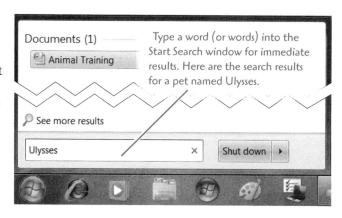

Type a word (or words) into the Start Search window for immediate results. Here are the search results for a pet named Ulysses.

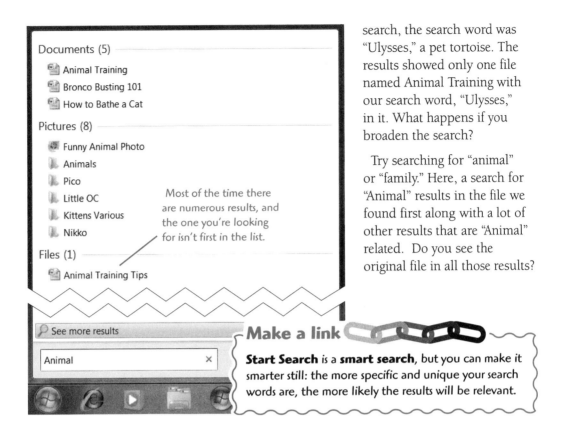

Documents (5)
- Animal Training
- Bronco Busting 101
- How to Bathe a Cat

Pictures (8)
- Funny Animal Photo
- Animals
- Pico
- Little OC
- Kittens Various
- Nikko

Most of the time there are numerous results, and the one you're looking for isn't first in the list.

Files (1)
- Animal Training Tips

See more results

Animal

Make a link

Start Search is a **smart search**, but you can make it smarter still: the more specific and unique your search words are, the more likely the results will be relevant.

search, the search word was "Ulysses," a pet tortoise. The results showed only one file named Animal Training with our search word, "Ulysses," in it. What happens if you broaden the search?

Try searching for "animal" or "family." Here, a search for "Animal" results in the file we found first along with a lot of other results that are "Animal" related. Do you see the original file in all those results?

What if the results you want *don't* appear in the Start menu's results list? If you accidentally saved a file to a temporary or system folder, or you can't think of any unique keywords to use when searching for it, or when you don't find what you want immediately, what do you do? You need to change your search strategy; you can either change your search words or perform a deeper search.

Filter the Start Search results list

What happens when you're looking for something and the item you're looking for doesn't appear in the Start Search results list? Click **See more results**. What happens?

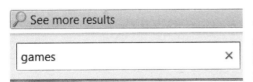

See more results

games

The results returned may include e-mail, documents, videos, folders, pictures, music, and any number of other items. If the list is too long, you need to filter the search results some more. How do you think you'd do that?

Select the **Details view**, and click a category like **Name**, **Date modified**, or **Type**.

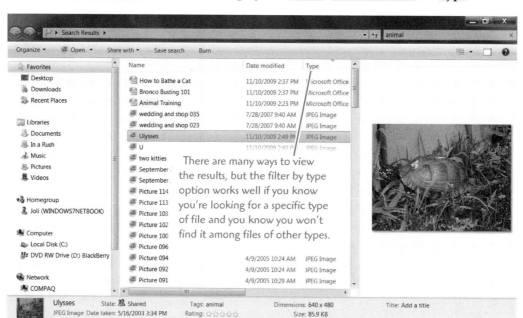

There are many ways to view the results, but the filter by type option works well if you know you're looking for a specific type of file and you know you won't find it among files of other types.

Did you notice the Preview pane's enabled? That lets you to preview any file in the results by clicking it *once*. Do you remember how to enable the preview pane if it's currently hidden? Click the icon next to **Change the View**. That icon is **Show the Preview Pane**.

Do you see what you want in the filtered results? If you don't really care where the item was, and you're just happy to find it, double-click it in the list of results to open it. Now you can save a copy of the file in the correct folder, view or play the file, or forward the e-mail to someone new.

But what if you do want to know where it was stored? Right-click the item and choose **Open File Location**. You may be surprised to find where the item was hiding.

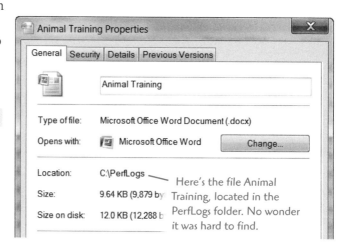

Here's the file Animal Training, located in the PerfLogs folder. No wonder it was hard to find.

What if you *still* don't see the item you're looking for or there are way too many results to look through? You need to filter those results some more. But where are the categories? They're not listed like they were in the Detail view. If the categories aren't listed, how will you apply filters?

Click inside the search box to **select a filtering option**. You can search by date modified, type, size, and name, for instance.

Select a filter, try Type, and scroll through the list of options to choose the type of data you're looking for. You can really be specific here, by searching only e-mail, audio files, playlists, and so on.

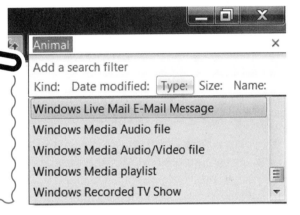

Make a link

If you don't see what you need, you need to **See more results**, and get a more **detailed view** or even **filter** those results by category. You can even **filter** right from the **search box** if you know what kind of search you want to perform.

Taskbar improvements

Do you miss Quick Launch? Does everything on the Taskbar look like it's all running together? And why are some the icons on the Taskbar indented while others aren't? And talking of icons . . . what *are* those new icons in the Notification Area?

Don't worry, everything's still available. Although the Taskbar's been improved, much of what you see on the Taskbar is familiar; there are still icons for open windows and programs, you still have access to the Start button, and the Notification Area is still on the right side. And of course, you can still access the clock and the date. But what about all the new stuff you can't see?

Open a few programs, like Windows Live Photo Gallery, a Windows Explorer window (like Documents), and a window for Help and Support. What happens to the Taskbar? Do the icons for the programs that are open look different from the icons for the programs that are not open?

Which programs are not open in the screenshot below? Which programs are open? How can you tell? What happens if you hover the cursor over the icon for any of the open programs?

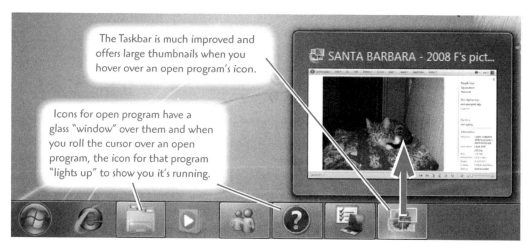

Pin items to the Taskbar

Do you want quick access to programs, games, and folders you use often, without cluttering up your desktop with shortcuts or having to go through the Start menu? What you really want is your old Quick Launch toolbar. While you can get that back (Google for the solution), you can obtain the same results by "pinning" items to the Taskbar.

One way to **pin an item to the Taskbar** is to locate it in the Start menu. Once you find the program you want to pin, here that's Remote Desktop Connection, right-click its icon in the menu. Choose **Pin to Taskbar** from the pop-up menu. Pin a couple more of your favorite programs and folders to the Taskbar. Now you can use the icon to launch the program or open the folder real quick.

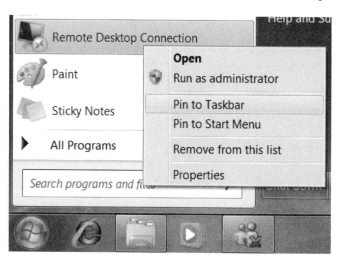

Once your items are pinned to the Taskbar, you can arrange their icons in whatever order you choose by dragging them to different places in the icon list.

Media Player's Jump List offers a list of recently played media. Notice how the active icon is lit up.

Take advantage of Jump Lists

The icons for programs on the Taskbar each offer a unique list of commands. Right-click any icon on the Taskbar to view its **Jump List**. What happens? Try a different icon. What happens this time?

What you see on the Jump List depends on the program and your recent activity with it. For instance, the Jump List in Media Player offers recent playlists you've accessed, along with recent songs and albums.

Media Center's Jump List offers access to the TV Program Guide, recently viewed videos, and even recorded TV.

Play with it

Here are a few ways you could save time with Jump Lists from Taskbar icons:

→ In the Jump Lists for Paint, Word, Notepad, PowerPoint, and so on: Select a file under Recent, click the File, then click Open. This means you can open the file without having to open the program first.

→ Use Media Player or Media Center's Jump Lists to select recently played media and play it again.

→ The Jump List for Internet Explorer lets you select a recently accessed website or start an InPrivate Browsing session.

→ Windows Live Messenger's Jump List gives you options to send an instant message, change your status, or go to your e-mail inbox.

→ Use the Windows Explorer window Jump List to access frequently accessed folders.

→ Windows Live Mail's Jump List lets you access recently viewed e-mails.

Which Jump Lists do you find most useful? How will they save you time?

Remove items from the Notification Area and stop alerts and notifications

You're happily cruising along, working, surfing, listening to music, or playing a game and minding your own business when it starts. Pop-ups from the Notification area. There are pop-ups for everything, from new mail to Windows updates, to network information. It's working your nerves and you'd like it to stop. Soon.

Luckily you can **stop notifications** and even **remove unwanted icons from the Notification area**.

1. Right-click an empty area of the Taskbar and click **Properties**.

2. From the Taskbar tab, under Notification area, click **Customize**. What happens?

Make a link

Change the **Taskbar Properties**.

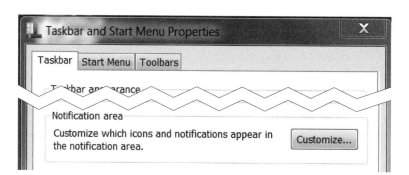

3. You have three choices for the notifications for each icon:

   a. Show icon and notifications.

   b. Hide icon and notifications.

   c. Only show notifications.

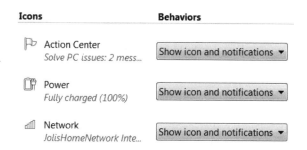

4. Make your selections and click OK. You can always come back here if you decide you *do* want notifications turned on for a specific icon.

5. While the Taskbar and Start Menu Properties dialog box is still open, make any changes you need to. You'll see familiar options including:

   a. Lock the taskbar.

   b. Auto-hide the taskbar.

   c. Use small icons.

6. If you want to change the **location** of the Taskbar from the bottom of the screen to the left, right, or top, you do that in the Taskbar and Start Menu Properties dialog box.

7. Configure how to group and label Taskbar icons when the Taskbar is full.

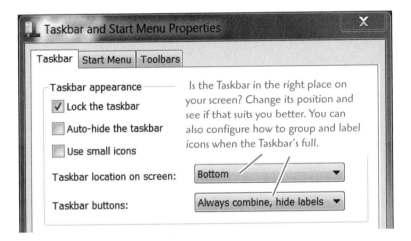

8. You can even **disable Aero Peek**, which allows you to hover your mouse over the rectangle to the right of the Notification Area to view the Desktop as it appears under any windows you have open.

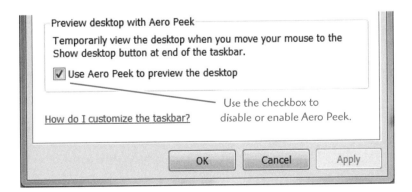

Reduce interruptions

Even though you've disabled notifications in the Notification Area, do you still feel like you're wasting time performing tasks you shouldn't have to perform? Or worse, do you feel like you spend quite a bit of time doing (or redoing or undoing) what should be done automatically or shouldn't have happened in the first place?

→ Do you have to manually connect to your wireless network each time you boot the computer?

→ Are you still being asked to input credentials or verify it's OK to make them when making system-wide changes?

→ And what about those new features? They were great in chapter 1 when Windows 7 was all shiny and new, but what if instead of improving your workflow some of the new features are slowing you down. Can you fix that?

→ When you insert an audio CD, does it play in iTunes when you'd like it to play in Media Player?

→ And is there a better way to open the Start menu without having to move your mouse to the Start button (especially if you're using a touchpad on a laptop).

Good news: you can personalize Windows 7 to reduce these interruptions and make the PC work more like *you* want it to.

Automatically connect to networks

Do you lose precious time every morning inputting your passcode or security key when you connect to your home or office network? How much time would it save if your computer could connect automatically anytime you're in range of the network?

To automatically connect to a trusted wireless network:

1. Open the **Network and Sharing Center**. (If you don't remember how, what could you type in the Start Search window?)

2. Click **Manage wireless networks**.

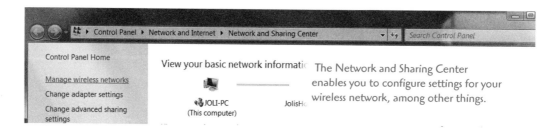

The Network and Sharing Center enables you to configure settings for your wireless network, among other things.

3. Double-click the network you want to connect to automatically when in range.

4. In the new dialog box, check **Connect automatically when this network is in range**.

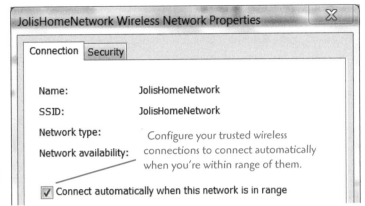

JolisHomeNetwork Wireless Network Properties

Connection | Security

Name: JolisHomeNetwork

SSID: JolisHomeNetwork

Network type:

Network availability:

Configure your trusted wireless connections to connect automatically when you're within range of them.

☑ Connect automatically when this network is in range

Disable Snap

If you're the kind of person who moves open windows around a lot and you've gotten used to manually positioning the windows, Snap—the feature that automatically arranges a window when you move it to the edge of the screen—can be a real pain. If you don't like it, you can turn off Snap.

1. Type "Snap" in the Start Search window.

2. Click **Turn off automatic window arrangement** in the results list.

3. In the dialog that appears, check **Prevent windows from being automatically arranged when moved to the edge of the screen**.

Make it easier to manage windows

☐ Activate a window by hovering over it with the mouse

☑ Prevent windows from being automatically arranged when moved to the edge of the screen

4. After you click OK, the Ease of Access Center options are available. Browse through the options. Do you see any other ways to make your computer easier to use?

Change user account control settings

User Account Control (UAC) is a safeguard and security feature in Windows 7. UAC prompts you to input Administrator credentials (or verify the action) when making system-wide changes to your computer. Most of the time *you're* the one making the change, but sometimes attempts to change system-related settings can be the result of a hacker, rogue program, or Internet-related threat.

Do you want to disable all of these notifications and reduce interruptions? But if you do that, even though you're pretty computer-literate, could your system be under threat?

Luckily, there's a range of notification options so you don't have to decide between always getting notification, or never getting them.

To make a change to UAC:

1. Click Start and type UAC.

2. In the results, click **Change User Account Control Settings**.

3. Select the desired setting and click OK.

Which of these four UAC options suits you and your workflow?

You can opt to turn off most notifications (or all of them).

Always notify	You're notified before programs make changes to your computer or to Windows settings that require administrator credentials. During the notification process, the Desktop is dimmed, and is thus "secure." No other program can run while the Desktop is in this secure mode. This is good for security, but bad for productivity because you have to stop what you're doing and deal with the notification.
Notify me only when programs try to make changes to my computer	This option also alerts you when a program outside of Windows tries to make changes to a Windows setting. You are not notified when you make changes to Windows settings that require administrator credentials.
Notify me only when programs try to make changes to my computer (do not dim my desktop)	As above, but this option doesn't dim your Desktop nor does it notify you on the secure Desktop.
Never notify	If you're logged on as an administrator you won't be notified about anything. Programs can make changes to your computer without you knowing about it. If you're logged on as a standard user, changes that require administrator approval are denied, and no notifications are offered.

Use keyboard shortcuts

If you're a laptop user and you find it difficult to use the touchpad, do you carry an external mouse with you? Even on a desktop PC, reaching for the mouse slows you down. You can work faster if you learn a few keyboard shortcuts.

Make a link

Win+Space — See your **Windows space**

Makes all **windows transparent** so you can see the desktop

Win+T — Take a scroll through the **Windows T**askbar

Press to **scroll** through the items on the **Taskbar**

Win+P — Changes **Windows P**resentation settings

Adjusts **Presentation** settings for your **display**

Shift+Click — A new kind of click that opens a new instance of a program

Used on a **taskbar item** opens a **new instance** of that program

Win+G — **G**adgets trump other **Windows**

Brings **Gadgets** to the front of open windows

Win+X — Turn off: **X**
Like the editing shortcut, Ctrl+X, but cuts off stuff on your whole **Windows** machine

Opens the **Mobility Center** to **turn off wireless** and perform other mobility tasks

Win+F — Finds stuff on your **Windows** machine

Opens a Search window so you can **Find** files and folders

Win+Tab — **Tab** through your open **Windows**

Use **Flip 3-D** to scroll through open windows

Do you remember any keyboard shortcuts from past operating systems? Try them now. Are there any that still work? Explore *possible* shortcuts while you're using programs. For instance, Alt+P opens the Play menu in Windows Media Player; in Excel, Ctrl+P opens the Print dialog box. Try similar key combinations with the letters S, D (try Win+D), and V with various applications open on the Desktop.

Change AutoPlay Settings

Do pictures from your digital camera open in the program you want them to? Or do they open in something you don't want, like Paint? What about your MP3 files? Do they play in iTunes when you'd really like them to play in Media Center or Media Player? You can fix that.

1. Click **Start > Default Programs**. There are four options, but the best place to start is to associate file types with specific programs.

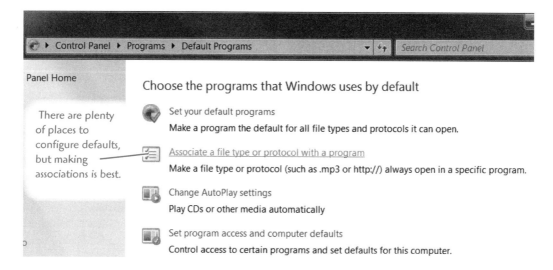

2. In the **Set Associations** window, find the type of file that currently opens in the wrong application. A few common file types you may want to change are listed below.

File extension	File type	Default program	Programs that will also open it
.aac	audio file	Media Player	QuickTime
.aiff	audio file	Media Player	iTunes, Live Movie Maker, or QuickTime
.avi	video file	Windows Media Player	Windows Media Center, QuickTime, Live Photo Gallery, Live Movie Maker, and others

File extension	File type	Default program	Programs that will also open it
.bmp	bitmap image file	Usually opens in Windows Live Photo Gallery.	Windows Live Photo Gallery, Paint, Media Center, and others
.gif	image file	Often opens in Internet Explorer	Windows Live Photo Gallery, Paint, Media Center, and others
.jpeg .jpg	image file	Usually opens in Windows Live Photo Gallery	Paint, Media Center, and others
.mpeg .mpg	video file	Windows Media Player	Windows Media Center, QuickTime, Live Photo Gallery, Live Movie Maker, and others
.mp3 .mp4	media file	Media Player	Windows Media Center, QuickTime, Live Photo Gallery, Live Movie Maker, and others
.tiff	image file	Usually opens in Windows Live Photo Gallery	Windows Live Photo Gallery, Paint, Media Center, and others
.txt	text document	Notepad	WordPad, Internet Explorer, and others
.wma	Windows Media Audio file	Media Player	Media Center

Your list will vary depending on what you have installed.

3. To set an association, select the file type, click **Change**, and select the desired program.

- -

Take a break

It's time to take a break. Take some time, walk away and give your brain some much needed time away from learning new things. This is a great time to go for a walk or catch up with that pile of mail sitting on the corner of your desk. When you're ready, come back for the Review and Experiment to test your newly learned skills.

Review

○ The Start Search window lets you type keywords to locate related data on your computer. It's best to use keywords that are unique (like "Ulysses"), versus those that are general (like "Animal"). Results appear in the Start menu's results list in categories including:

→ ....

→ Pictures

→ ....

→ ....

→ Programs

→ Control Panel

○ You can click any item in the list to ....

○ The Search Results window, available when you click ....
.... from the Start menu after searching for data in it, offers many ways to filter the results:

→ Change the view options to .... to access column names like Name, Date modified, Type, Folder, and more. Click the headings to .... data in those columns alphabetically, by .... or by ....

→ In the Search window, click to view .... options, including kind, date modified, type, size, and name. Once a filter is selected, you can further cull the data by selecting a specific .... of data.

→ Show the .... pane to view a thumbnail of the data before committing to opening it. This allows you to browse more quickly through the results.

→ Right-click any result to view .... for it, including .... file location. If you know similar files are stored in that location, you may be able to open the location to locate the missing data.

↻ You can perform new tasks with the Taskbar:

→ You can .... and then .... Taskbar icons.

→ You can .... notifications from the ....
and remove unwanted icons.

→ You can .... any icon to view its Jump List and perform
application-specific tasks. It's best if the application is open.

→ The Taskbar .... dialog box lets you move the
....

↻ There are several ways to reduce interruptions and make the computer
easier to use:

→ Configure your computer to .... connect to wireless
networks you trust.

→ .... features like Snap, that can throw you off if you
aren't used to them.

→ Change UAC settings so you aren't always asked for ....
.... when making changes to your computer.

→ Learn .... for performing common tasks
without taking your hands off the keyboard.

→ Change autoplay settings so that the proper programs open when
you .... or ....

How did you do?

Did you forget anything? It's hard to remember it all.
Go ahead and re-read the sections covering what you
overlooked. Your brain might need a bit more time to
absorb all the information. Be sure to make strong and
vivid links to the information.

Experiment

The best way to really cement these features and techniques into your long-term memory is to try out some of these features on your own. Here are some suggestions for experiments that use techniques covered in this chapter.

Perform an advanced search and save it

Think of something you store on your computer that's unique and special to you. Perhaps you have lots of pictures of your kids and have added tags or file names that represent them; you have a company name that's unique, or you have data related to a hobby. Type a word related to that in the Start Search window, and click See more results.

Configure your screen like this:

1. Change the view to Details.

2. Click Type to sort the list by file type.

3. Show the preview pane.

4. Click any item once in the results list to view it.

Here are some other helpful Search tips:

→ Change Folder Options so that the search also looks through the files names and contents of the files. This will make the results more complete.

→ If the search results offer partial matches you aren't interested in, in Folder Options remove the check by Find partial matches.

→ To review the search results at another time, click Save search. The Save search feature is more useful in creating "live" folders though. For instance, you can perform a search for a specific word, like "widget", save the search, and every time you open the folder, new results will appear, based on the current status of related data.

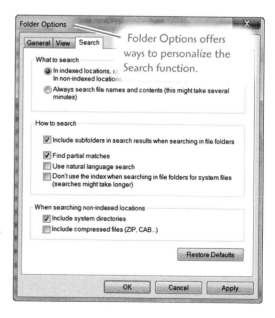

Folder Options offers ways to personalize the Search function.

→ Now, click Save Search. Name the search descriptively, and save it in a place you can find it later!

File name: Ballew search results

Save as type: Saved Search

Authors: Joli   Tags: Add a tag

Note: The results in the **all results** list don't actually show "all" of the results, but they should provide the information you need. For instance, by default, the search will look in indexed locations, but in non-indexed locations it'll also search file names (but not what's in the file). This allows the search to go faster. Search also won't look in ZIP or CAB files, these are compressed files. You can change this behavior later if you still don't find what you want.

Indexed locations include all of your libraries, e-mail, and offline files. Non-indexed files include program and system files, which don't usually contain user-created data.

You can change search behavior from the Organize button in the Search Results window.

AutoPlay and Default Programs

The other three options in the Default Programs window are:

→ Set your default programs

→ Change AutoPlay Setting

→ Set program access and computer defaults

Experiment with these options. Consider how the following changes would alter your workflow:

→ Do you like Media Center over Media Player? Click **Set your default programs**, click Windows Media Center and choose **Set this program as default**.

→ Do you connect external hardware, like an iPhone? You can configure the device to do what you want when you connect it. Click **AutoPlay** in the control panel. Now you can just let your iPhone **Open device to view files using Windows Explorer** instead of **Ask me every time**.

→ If you often listen to audio CDs, in **AutoPlay**, select **Play audio CD using Windows Media Player** or another option like **Import songs using iTunes**.

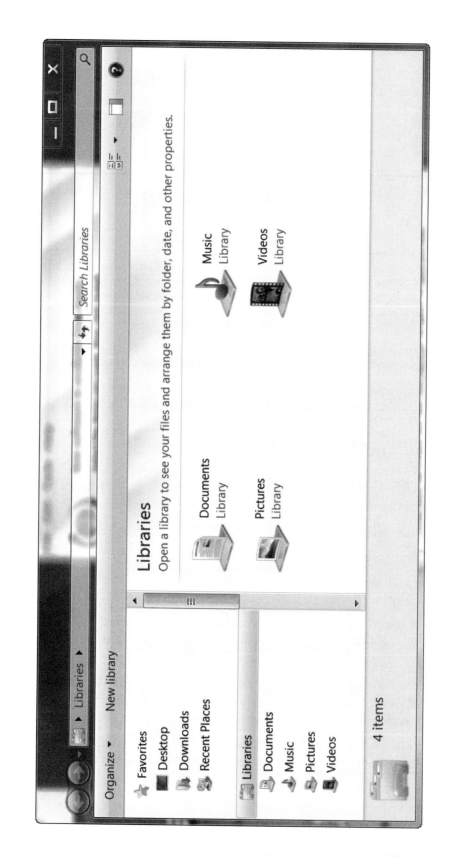

9 Organize data with Libraries

You're tired of browsing to network folders; you're losing time accessing folders on your external hard drive; "exploring" for the files you've saved in folders outside of the Windows 7 defaults is a pain. You need a way to access and manage this data efficiently.

⇨ There's data you use *often* on your computer's hard drive.

⇨ There are backups and *rarely* used data on an external drive.

⇨ There's data in default folders on networked computers you *sometimes* need to access.

⇨ There's a combination of data in folders you've created for the purpose of keeping files related to a single topic, client, hobby, or project together.

No Problem!

Windows Libraries are the answer to all your data management problems. There are four Libraries: Documents, Music, Videos, and Pictures, and they automatically gather content from built-in folders on your computer and offer an easy way to access that data.

⇨ Windows Libraries work like libraries in the real world. They monitor your folders and collect together related information. Each library displays related data in one single window.

⇨ By default, the Windows 7 Libraries monitor your personal folders as well as public ones. But you can configure any Library to monitor a folder on a networked computer, external drive, and even some USB flash drives. You can tell a Library to monitor folders on your hard drive too.

How do Libraries work?

You know how a library in the real world works, right? Well, **Windows Libraries** work in kind of the same way. They monitor your folders and collect together related information. When you open a library it displays links to all the related data in one single window; no more trawling through loads of subfolders, just immediate access to your data. But how do Windows Libraries work?

Without you having to do anything, your Libraries have already started collecting links to your data. Open your personal folder and browse what's in your Libraries already:

1. Click the folder icon on the Taskbar. Do you see your Libraries? There are four libraries by default; Documents, Music, Pictures, and Videos.

    The folder icon in the Taskbar opens your Libraries.

2. Click the **Videos Library**. The Library shown here contains links to the Windows 7 sample videos, a vacation video from a digital camera, an AVI file from a different digital video camera, and more.

    How can you tell what program the videos are configured to play in?

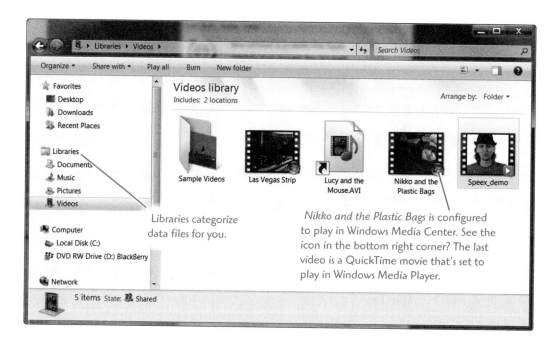

Libraries categorize data files for you.

Nikko and the Plastic Bags is configured to play in Windows Media Center. See the icon in the bottom right corner? The last video is a QuickTime movie that's set to play in Windows Media Player.

Your personal Videos folder only shows you the videos you've saved there. If you've got videos saved in the Public Videos folder as well, that's two places you have to keep track of. Wouldn't it be great if there were something that could keep track for you and display all your videos in one place?

Take another look at the Videos Library window. Under the Videos Library title, what do you think **Includes: 2 Locations** means?

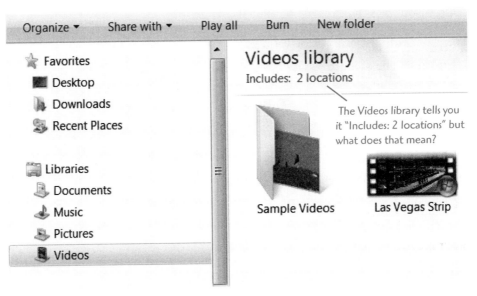

By default, Libraries gather their content from two locations: your personal folder and the Public folder with a corresponding name.

The **Videos Library** monitors the data stored in both the Videos and the Public Videos folders. Now there's no need to check the Videos folder *and* the Public Videos folder, the Videos Library shows you what's in both in a single window.

Use Libraries for data management

Create a folder called BookCrossing on your Desktop (right-click and choose New > Folder). You want to create the folder outside of the folders that the Libraries already monitor, which include your personal folders and the Public folders.

Go online and do a search for BookCrossing. Save something (an image or document, perhaps) that contains information about BookCrossing in your new folder. You can right-click the BookCrossing logo and click Save Picture As, for instance. Or, you could search for BookCrossing PDF, and when prompted to Find or Save to document, click Save. Just make sure to save to your new BookCrossing folder in either instance.

Open your personal folder again and take a look in the Libraries for your new BookCrossing data. If you saved a picture, it is in your Pictures Library? If you saved a document, is it in your Documents Library? Can you think of a way to get the data in your BookCrossing folder to show up in the Libraries?

By default, Libraries only gather data from your folders and Public folders, but you can configure any Library to monitor and include a specific folder on your hard drive:

1. Open your personal folder again, if necessary. In the left-hand pane of the window, right-click **Documents** in the Library list and select **Properties**.

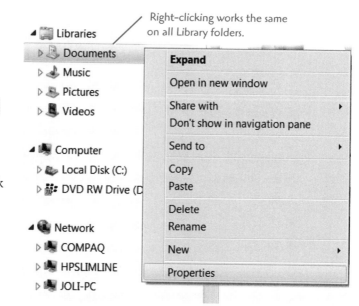

2. In the Documents Properties dialog, click **Include a folder**, and browse to the location of the folder to add; here you need to browse to the folder you created on the Desktop.

3. Click **Include folder**. The BookCrossing folder appears in the Library Properties dialog box.

4. Click OK.

The Properties dialog box for any Library offers a place to include a folder and to show the locations already being monitored.

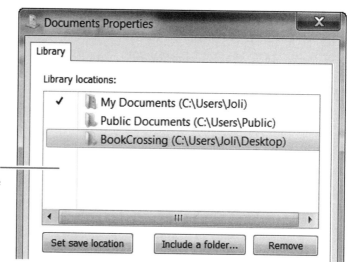

Re-open the Documents Library folder. What do you see this time? How many Locations are included now? Scroll down to locate the new Library.

▴ BookCrossing (2)
C:\Users\Joli\Desktop

BookCrossing-in-the-Classroom.pdf   11/12/2009 1:28 PM   PDF File

BookCrossing   11/12/2009 1:19 PM   JPEG Image

Make a link

Libraries offer access to the **data** you've saved to your **default folders**, as well as data in your **Public folders**, all from a single window.

Libraries can be **configured** to monitor areas of your hard drive and personal folders **outside of the default folders**.

The Documents Library now collects information about documents you've saved in the Documents folder, the Public Documents folder, and your BookCrossing folder on the Desktop, but the BookCrossing folder contains images as well or maybe even some video. Adding the BookCrossing folder to each of these Libraries is fine for this folder, but manually adding every folder you create outside of the folders the Libraries monitor by default is going to get old fast.

Say you've found a BookCrossing book, written a review of it for your local paper and saved the review in a subfolder called "BookReviews" in a folder called "Work" that's saved outside the default Document folders. Logically that review belongs under "Work" because you got paid for it, but it also belongs with your other BookCrossing information. What do you do? Creating a copy of the document will just fill up your hard drive . . .

You can fix both of these problems. What you need is a BookCrossing Library to keep BookCrossing-related information together, regardless of its location.

Create your own Libraries

You've created the folders you need, and stored them where you want them, and now you need to create a new Library to monitor them.

To create your own Library and define what should be part of it, open the Libraries folder and click **New library**. You did see the option to create a new library, didn't you?

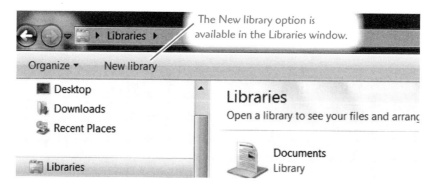

The New library option is available in the Libraries window.

Right-click the new Library icon that appears and give your new library a name; we'll call this one BookCrossing. You're ready to configure it. Double-click your Library to open it. How many Locations are included?

When you create a Library, by default, no folders are included. You need to add folders to monitor and include. How will you add your two folders (BookCrossing and BookReviews) to the locations your BookCrossing Library gathers information from? Hint: you already know how to **Include** locations. After you've added the folders to include, your new Library is ready.

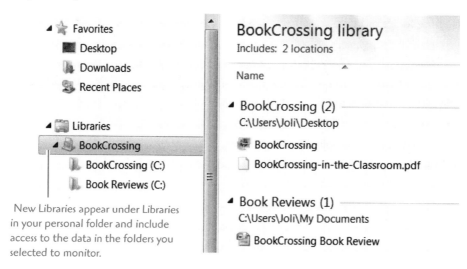

New Libraries appear under Libraries in your personal folder and include access to the data in the folders you selected to monitor.

Libraries are also useful if you need to gather together references from a bunch of places temporarily. Say you're doing a project that needs reference material from one folder, images from another, and so on, but you don't want to move those files or copy them because it would fill up your hard drive.

Make a link

When you **create** a **new Library**, no data is moved there. You're only creating "links" to the data you need.

Creating a Library to get access to them is a great solution! And when you're done, it makes sense to delete the Library, but what happens when you delete it? Think about it . . .

Tip: Sometimes when you install a new third-party program it creates its own folder during installation. Later, when you're using the program any data you create is stored in the program's folder by default. If you're not comfortable changing those settings, or if you've made changes but the program keeps reverting to them, Libraries can help.

Configure a Library to offer access to a third-party program's proprietary folder. Find out what the folder name is (My Graphics, My Greeting Cards, My Resumes, or something similar), and where it's stored on the hard drive (the C: drive or a folder in it), then add that folder to a Library for easier access to the files it contains.

Use Search inside a Library folder

Open a Library folder that contains several subfolders like Documents, Music, or Pictures. In the Search box, type a word that represents a piece of data available there. Review the results. Click inside the Search window again, and add criteria. Review the results once more.

Libraries offer another way to search, too. If you can't recall where a specific file is stored, but you're sure it's not in the folder it would logically be in, you can look in Libraries.

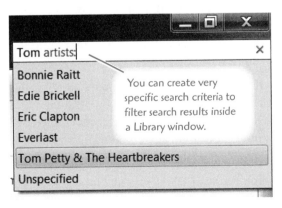

You can create very specific search criteria to filter search results inside a Library window.

Say you want to locate a picture you took while you were on vacation, but it's not in the Pictures folder or in the Vacations subfolder you created to put all your vacation photos in.

Maybe the photo's in a subfolder of Documents, because you inserted it into another article for the local paper. To find out if you're right, click the Documents Library and search for "JPEG image."

Libraries offer a way to search through folders and subfolders to locate elusive files.

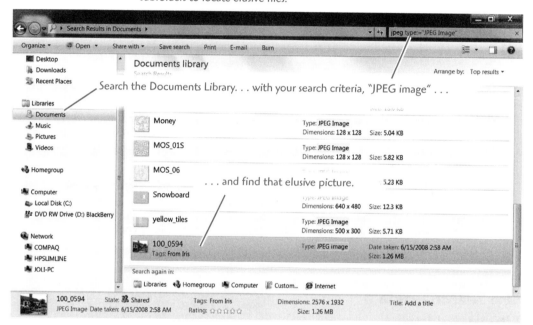

Add an external drive or network share

Say you've archived the BookCrossing folder from your Desktop to a networked PC (perhaps even putting it in another folder called Backups), but you still need to access the folder occasionally. If the folder you moved it to is already being monitored by your current Libraries, you'll still have access to it. How does that work?

If your network settings are configured to allow Public Folder Sharing, and you put the BookCrossing folder in a Public folder, or if you moved the BookCrossing folder to a networked folder that's already been included in a Library, the folder and its contents would show up in any Libraries that monitor those locations.

However, if (after the move) the data doesn't appear in any Library, or you want it to appear in your BookCrossing Library, you'll have to add the network location.

You can create a link to a shared folder on another computer in any Library, so this will work great for your BookCrossing Library folder:

1. Open your personal folder and open the Library you'd like to add the network share to. Here, that's the BookCrossing Library.

2. Right-click anywhere that's blank inside the Library window and select **Properties**.

3. Click **Include a folder**.

4. Navigate to the location of the shared folder.

5. Click **Include folder**, and then OK.

Tip: Libraries can even access data on networked computers, external hard drives, and even some USB drives.

Re-open your personal folder from the Taskbar's Windows Explorer icon and click the BookCrossing Library. The folder on the network drive will show up (as long as the networked computer's turned on) and you can locate files and folders on it as easily as you could if they were on your PC.

▲ BookCrossing (2)
C:\Users\Joli\Desktop

☐ BookCrossing-in-the-Classroom.pdf

⊞ BookCrossing

Before: the BookCrossing Library was placed on the Desktop.

▲ BookCrossing (2)
\\HPSLIMLINE\Users\Joli\Desktop

⊞ BookCrossing

☐ BookCrossing-in-the-Classroom.pdf

After: the BookCrossing library has been moved to a networked folder that isn't monitored by any of the default libraries, so you need to create a link to a network share. (Note the path is on a networked computer named HPSLIMLINE.)

Take a break

Phew! That was a vault of information. Give your brain a break. Go do something else for a while. Got a magazine to read? Need to check your e-mail? Do that now and we'll see you back here in 10, rested and ready to review, then dive in and Experiment to cement these new skills in your brain.

Review

○ Libraries .... information about the data on your computer, and offer access to all related files from there. A Library doesn't .... the data, though, it only offers a place to access it. If a document was saved in a folder called Clients on the C: drive, it'll remain there.

○ You can .... access to that file from the Documents Library. Libraries can also be configured to monitor data on .... drives and ...., external ...., and even some USB flash drives.

○ You can use Libraries in a number of ways:

→ To .... specific types of data quickly.

→ To locate .... files.

→ To .... data better.

→ To access data on .... drives, some USB flash drives, and folders that aren't part of the Windows 7 .... folders.

→ You can create your own .... to manage data specific to you.

How did you do?

Did you forget anything? It's hard to remember it all. Go ahead and re-read the sections covering what you overlooked. Your brain might need a bit more time to absorb all the information.

Experiment

The best way to really cement these features and techniques into your long-term memory is to expand on the techniques you just learned about by using them and taking them just one step further. Be sure to bring in things you've learned in previous chapters as well, if that helps you work through the experiment.

Access data on a flash drive

Plug in a new USB flash drive, if you have one. Put some data on the drive. See if you can configure a Library to monitor what's on the drive. Some newer USB drives are compatible.

Explore Libraries and Library Views

Open your personal folder and click the **Pictures Library**.

→ From the View icon on the toolbar, select **Extra Large Icons**.

→ Next, select **Details**. Right-click the column heading and select More. From the resulting Choose Details dialog box, select the details you'd like to see. For the Pictures Library consider photo-related entries like Lens maker, Lens model, Camera maker, or Camera model, if any of these interest you.

→ You can further sort the data in any Library (in Details view) by clicking one of these column headings. Click **Name** to order the results alphabetically. Click it again to reverse the order.

→ Click **Date modified** to view the results by the dates they were last changed (and click it again to reverse the order) or click Type to view results by their type.

Joli
Administrator
Password protected

Cosmo
Standard user
Password protected

Johnny Junior
Standard user
Password protected

Administrator
Administrator
Password protected

Jennifer
Standard user
Password protected

Guest
Guest account

Create a new account

What is a user account?

Additional things you can do

 Set up Parental Controls

Go to the main User Accounts page

10

User accounts secure your computer

⇨ Do you have kids that use the same PC you do? Do they install programs, get into your personal data, or use the computer in the middle of the night when they're supposed to be sleeping?

⇨ Have you shared data on your network, only to find that some of your family members can't access the data at all? Or worse they have to use *your* user name and password to gain access? That means they can see your personal data.

⇨ Have you ever had a guest visit and need to use your computer to get their e-mail, check their flight status, and access your word processing program? It seems innocent enough at the time, but after they've gone you find they also installed software and downloaded games onto your PC without your permission. They even changed your Desktop background!

There has to be a better way to let people use your computer or network without letting them see all your personal data or private folders . . .

No Problem!

The solutions to all these problems are simple. You need to create user accounts and configure the kind of data sharing you want.

Which user account is best?

You need to allow other people access to your PC but you want to control what they can and can't install, what times they can and can't log on, and what programs they can and can't use. How can creating another user account solve all those problems?

The solution involves creating user accounts. But there are different kinds of user accounts. Which account is right for which situation? And how could user accounts help you share data over a network?

→ To allow children (or other relatives) access to your PC while also controlling what they can and can't install, what times they can and can't log on, and what programs they can and can't use, create *password-protected Standard user accounts* for each of them and apply parental controls. (Yes, you can apply parental controls to adult accounts!)

→ To allow physical access to your PC without also offering access to your personal data, create *password-protected Standard user accounts* for each user you want to allow access to. Apply a password to your account if you don't have one.

→ To allow a guest that visits often to access your computer to check their e-mail or use your word processing program (and to store data), create a *password-protected Standard user account* for them. For the occasional visitor, simply enable the Guest account that comes with Windows 7 when they arrive.

> **Warning**
> Be careful with the Guest account. Don't enable it before you need to and *disable it as soon as your guests leave*; it's a haven for malware, as many bits of unwelcome software target the Guest and Administrator accounts.

→ To allow others on your network to access shared data like music and photos from other PCs, and to minimize problems that arise when accessing that data, turn on Media Sharing, Public Folder Sharing, and/or File and Printer Sharing and/or create a user account for them on your PC.

You probably know already how easy it is to create a user account: you just work through a few wizard pages. But what kinds of accounts can you create, what type should you choose, and for whom?

There are only two types of accounts that you can create (there's a Guest account, too, but that's already been created): Administrator and Standard user.

Who's the Administrator?

Joli
Administrator
Password protected

The **Administrator account** should be reserved only for the person who will manage and be responsible for the computer.

→ *You are the administrator of your computer*, unless you know for certain that someone else is.

→ The Administrator account is the account you set up during the Windows 7 initialization process. It's the account that lets you configure your PC and install programs.

→ There must be at least one Administrator account per computer.

→ The administrator can do anything they want, including changing security settings, installing software and hardware, and accessing all the files on the computer.

→ Administrators can also make changes to other user accounts.

What can Standard account users do?

Jennifer
Standard user
Password protected

A **Standard account** is less powerful and gives users only certain rights.

→ Standard users can access and use installed programs, create files and folders, personalize their Desktop, Taskbar, and Start menu, access any data in the Public folders, and do just about anything else an Administrator can do.

→ If a Standard user tries to install software, hardware, change security settings, make changes to user accounts, or otherwise attempt to perform a task that will affect other users who have access to the computer, they may be prompted to input an administrator's name and password.

→ Crucially there are a few things you *can't* do with a Standard account, like change User Account Control (UAC) settings, but not so many that it makes using a Standard account inefficient or troublesome.

Standard user account safety features

Standard user accounts are inherently safer than Administrator accounts. Standard users can't cause much harm to the computer because, to make system-wide changes, they have to ask for an Administrator's permission in the form of the Administrator's name and password. The Standard user must enter that information before the computer will apply any changes. So if a threat arrives from the Internet while a Standard user is logged on, theoretically it can't do as much harm to the PC as it could if an Administrator was logged on instead. It has to do with the permissions a user is granted.

Warning
Microsoft suggests you use the account created during setup as your Administrator account, then create a Standard user account for everyday computing tasks. For safety's sake, you'll learn how to do that later in the chapter, should you desire.

When you create a Standard user account for anyone, as the administrator of the computer you can apply parental controls. Parental controls aren't just for kids! Do you have a spouse that needs to get off the computer at 6 p.m. for dinner? Set time limits. Have a forgetful parent who can't remember if he should use Microsoft Word, WordPad, Notepad, or something else? Deny access to all programs but the ones he should use. Have teenagers that ignore game ratings? Block games that don't meet your criteria.

Who are the people who currently access or need to access your personal PC or the data on it? There are three scenarios:

1.	Users who physically access your personal PC	Create a password-protected Standard user account on your PC for each of these users.
2.	Users who have tried to access shared data on your PC but have been unable to log on to the PC when they try	Create a password-protected Standard user account on your PC for each of these users to immediately resolve this problem.
3.	Users on other networked PCs that you don't necessarily want to create a user account on your own PC for, but with whom you'd like to share data in your Public folders and printers	Change sharing options to allow these users to access shared data.

What users need access on your network? What types of accounts or sharing options do you think you'll want to create for them?

Create a user account for another user on your Windows 7 PC

Creating a password-protected Standard user account for your children (and anyone else who uses your computer) makes things easier for everyone. Once an account's been created and a password set, the user is protected from nosy brothers and sisters, relatives, or friends. Each user can personalize their own Desktop background, screen saver, and Taskbar, and add folders, data, shortcuts, or other data to the Desktop. But you still have control. You can set restrictions using Parental Controls, reset a lost password, share data using the computer's built-in Public folders, and more.

Once Standard accounts are set up for other users, you can rest easy too. As long as *your* user account is password-protected (and the other users don't know the password), no one can access your personal data, no matter how hard they try.

And finally, if each user who needs to access shared data on your PC has a password-protected user account on it, all of those annoying "Logon Unsuccessful" messages will be eliminated.

So you're ready to set up other people with their own user accounts, but where do you do that?

1. Click Start > Control Panel > **Add or remove user accounts**.

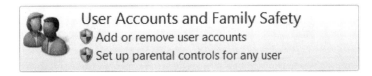

2. Click **Create a new account**.

3. Type a name for the new user, click **Standard User**, and click **Create Account**.

4. Click the new account in the Manage Accounts dialog to apply a password.

5. Click **Create a password**.

6. Type the password, type it again to confirm, type a password hint, then click **Create Password**.

Johnny Junior
Standard user

7. Click **Manage another account** to return to the main user accounts page. Do you see the new account? How do you know that it's password-protected?

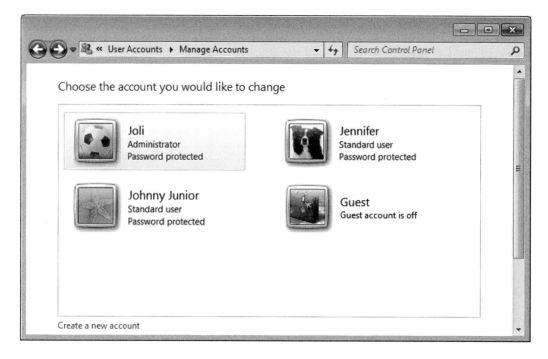

The next time you boot the PC, you'll see your account name and the new account name. The new user can now log on with their account. The first time they log on, the Desktop will look brand new, just like it did when you first brought the computer home. That new user will need to configure the Desktop, configure their e-mail program, and possibly connect to the network, and they may have to install cell phone software or other personalized applications only they need.

But what about programs everyone uses, like Windows Live, iTunes, Microsoft Office, and similar programs? Will the new user have access to those? Yes they will. Standard users have access to applications that have been installed and are shared, and won't need to reinstall those applications.

Can two people share a PC effectively?

Sharing a PC can be trying, right? How many times have you needed to access your PC but found someone else using it? Although there are no hard and fast rules, there are a few built-in features that make sharing a PC a bit easier.

Two users can be logged in at the same time

You need to access your PC to check your e-mail, but another user's using the PC. You each have user accounts, but you can't simply roll her away in her office chair, stand there for a few minutes and look at your e-mail (and then roll her back). And even if she stepped away to let you on, you can't access your "version" of Microsoft Outlook from her user account or the document you need to attach to the e-mail you need to send either. You need her to do one of the following:

- ☐ Turn off the computer so you can log on. This means she'll have to close all of her open programs—and she's in the middle of something, so she'll never agree to this option.

- ☐ Log off so that you can log on. She'll still have to close all of her programs so this option won't irritate her much less than the first one.

  Luckily you have a third option.

- ☐ Click Start, and click the arrow next to Shut down, then click **Switch user**. This lets you log on to your account but leaves other users logged on, all their programs running, and all their windows open. Now you can check your e-mail, and give her back the computer as soon as you're finished, which just might fly.

Switching users is fast, and allows multiple users to be logged on to the computer at the same time. Each user's open programs and windows remain open in the background. After the users are switched back, the first user will find her Desktop exactly the way she left it. (Although a wireless network connection may be disabled during the switch.)

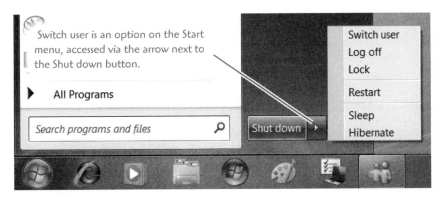

Switch user is an option on the Start menu, accessed via the arrow next to the Shut down button.

Play with it

Make Switch user the default setting on the Start menu (instead of Shut down)

If you and another person share a computer and you use Switch user a lot, wouldn't it be great if you could change the default Start menu option, Shut down, to Switch user?

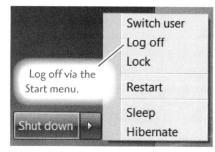

Taskbar and Start Menu Properties

| Taskbar | Start Menu | Toolbars |

To customize how links, icons, and menus look and behave in the Start menu, click Customize.

Power button action: [Switch user ▼]

1. Right-click the Start button and click **Properties**.

2. Under the Start menu tab, next to Power button action, select **Switch user**.

Log off completely to save resources

Switch users is pretty cool. Switching users is quick, and the Desktop looks the same when you switch back. It's perfect for quickly accessing your own account to perform a single task like reading your e-mail. But when a few people are logged on (and when those users each have multiple programs running), your computer reacts more slowly than it usually does. What gives?

Your computer uses resources to run several programs at the same time. If you have four programs running, another user has three, and still another user has six or eight, it's going to be hard for your computer to manage all of those open programs and it may run more slowly. Can you stop this happening?

It's best for users to completely log off when they're finished using the computer. When a user logs off, their programs and windows are closed, and the account is "shut down" though the computer remains turned on and ready for the next user. When a user's logged off, no programs are running in the background using up system resources. This makes the computer more responsive for the users that are still logged on. How do you log off?

Did you notice the **Log off** option when you found Switch user on the Start menu?

What happens when you click Lock, Sleep, or Hibernate, also found on the Start menu?

Make a link

Two or more users can be **logged on at the same time**, but it's best to log off to make sure the computer runs faster for the other users.

Switch user
Log off
Lock

Log off via the Start menu.

Restart

Shut down ▶

Sleep
Hibernate

The Guest account can serve as a temporary user account

Have you ever had a friend visit and need to use your PC to check flight times or keep on top of their e-mail? It seems innocent enough at the time, but the problem is that the last time your friend visited he installed iTunes and "authorized" your computer to download music to his iPod. You didn't even notice at the time until the endless nagging started. iTunes wanted you to install updates here and updates there. Ugh.

Well not this time. Nope. This time you're going to create a user account just for him, or perhaps even use the Guest account. The *what* account?

People using the **Guest** account can access data other members of the "User Group" can (think Standard users), including shared programs like Microsoft Office or Internet Explorer, and they can personalize the Desktop with a background, apply a screen saver, and access Public folders. But just like Standard users, they can't access other users' data, install programs (without inputting an Administrator name and password), or make changes to computer settings or user accounts.

Is the Guest account a better option than creating a Standard user account?

If you're only planning to use the account *for a short period of time* and will *disable it once it's no longer needed*, the Guest account can be a good option to allow occasional users access to your PC without going via your user account. The reason you should disable it as soon as you're done with it? The Guest account can be attacked by malware and viruses, just like any other account, and you shouldn't leave it enabled when no one is using it.

1. To minimize the steps involved in locating the Guest account, it's best to simply type Guest in the Start Search window. Click **Turn guest account on or off** in the results.

   Control Panel (1)

2. Click the Guest account and choose **Turn On**. When the computer boots, or when a user logs off, the Guest account will appear as a user account option. Guests should click **Guest** to log on.

Warning

There are a few things to know about the Guest account:

▶ As long as the Guest account is enabled, a user can log off and log back on to the PC using this account. The same Desktop background, screen saver, and other settings will be maintained. Even if the computer is rebooted, as long as the Guest account is enabled, the Guest account settings will be saved.

▶ Guests can save data to the hard drive, and, by default, that data is saved in the Guest account in the appropriate Library. Guests can access data in Public folders.

▶ Administrators can view a guest's saved data by logging on as an administrator and browsing to C:\Users\Guest, and then navigating through the Guest account Libraries. Standard users cannot access a Guest's data unless they input an Administrator name and password.

▶ If you turn off the Guest account and restart the computer, Guest is no longer an option at the log on screen.

▶ When you turn the Guest account back on, and a different user logs on using the Guest account, the settings from the last user are retained. The new Guest user will have the last Guest user's Desktop background, screen saver, and even have access to the last Guest user's saved data.

Apply parental controls to manage the amount of time a standard user can have on the PC

You've created a password-protected Standard user account, but what if you'd like to limit when that user can log on to the computer? To set time limits you'll need to apply **Parental Controls**:

1. Click Start > Control Panel, and under **User Accounts and Family Safety**, click **Set up parental controls for any user**.

2. Select the Standard user account that you want to set time limits on. (You can't apply parental controls to administrator accounts.)

3. Under Parental Controls, click **On**, enforce current settings.

4. Click **Time Limits**.

Note: If you impose time limits, users can't log on during the limited time. Every other account on the computer should be password-protected and the Guest account turned off.

Parental Controls: ─────────────
● On, enforce current settings
○ Off

Parental Controls let you define when a Standard user can and can't access the computer, among other things.

Current Settings:

Johnny Junior
Standard user
Password protected

Windows Settings

🕐 Time limits
Control when Johnny Junior uses the computer

🏆 Games
Control games by rating, content, or title

▦ Allow and block specific programs
Allow and block any programs on your computer

Time Limits: Off

Game Ratings: Off

Program Limits: Off

5. Drag the cursor over blocks of time in the grid provided to allow or block access.

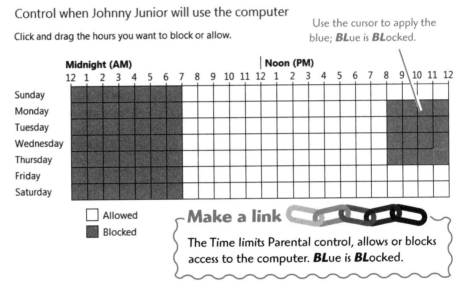

Control when Johnny Junior will use the computer

Click and drag the hours you want to block or allow.

Use the cursor to apply the blue; **BL**ue is **BL**ocked.

□ Allowed
▦ Blocked

⟋Make a link ⬭⬭⬭⬭

The Time limits Parental control, allows or blocks access to the computer. **BL**ue is **BL**ocked.

6. Click OK. (Be sure to click OK again before closing the Parental Controls window.)

Play with it

Create Parental Controls for what games a Standard user can play, and what programs they can use. If you have a teenager, consider applying a block for games that do not have ratings or those that are for adults only.

Johnny Junior
Standard user - Parental Controls On
Password protected

Resolve sharing issues on a network

If another user on your home network can't access the data stored on your PC from his computer, can you troubleshoot that? It could be one of many things (including the way sharing is set up) but most likely it's because the other user doesn't have a user account on your PC. If you create a Standard user account on your PC, it's fast, secure, and safe and it would resolve the problem immediately.

A Standard account should do the trick

You already know how to create Standard, password-protected, user accounts on your PC, so set one up now. Even if the other user never plans to log on to your PC, creating an account for him provides an immediate solution. Once you've created the account, on the other PC, try again to access the shared data. When prompted, type the new username and password. The issue should be resolved. (If it isn't, or if you really don't want to create additional accounts on your computer, work through the steps below.)

Check the Network and Sharing settings

There are other ways to resolve sharing issues without creating user accounts for those who need access, though. If you don't want a ton of accounts on your PC, try changing the sharing options.

To review and make changes to sharing settings:

1. In the Start Search window type "Network and Sharing." From the results, click **Network and Sharing Center**.

2. In the Network and Sharing Center, click **Change advanced sharing settings**.

3. Scroll through the options and verify these settings and/or make the following adjustments to resolve the sharing issues you're having:

Manage wireless networks

Change adapter settings

Change advanced sharing settings

Network discovery

When network discovery is on, this computer can see other network computers and devices and is visible to other network computers. What is network discovery?

◉ Turn on network discovery
○ Turn off network discovery

File and printer sharing

When file and printer sharing is on, files and printers that you have shared from this computer can be accessed by people on the network.

◉ Turn on file and printer sharing
○ Turn off file and printer sharing

Public folder sharing

When Public folder sharing is on, people on the access files in the Public folders. What are the Public folders?

If you don't want to create user accounts for those users on your network who need access to the data on your PC, change the default sharing options. Don't forget to click Save Changes!

◉ Turn on sharing so anyone with network access can read and write files in the Public folders
○ Turn off Public folder sharing (people logged on to this computer can still access these folders)

If network problems still persist, consider the issues and solutions outlined in this table...

Issue	No Problem!
Is the computer on the network?	In order for others to access your computer and the data on it **Network Discovery must be turned on.**
You want other users to be able to share files or share a printer, but they can't access the files or printer	To allow people on the network to access files and printers you have shared **File and Printer Sharing must be turned on**.
Users can't see data in the Public folders on your PC	In order for people on the network including HomeGroup members (see chapter 12) to access data in the Public folders on your PC **Public Folder Sharing must be turned on**.
Other users can't access the media on your PC	To allow access to the media stored on your personal PC **Media Streaming must be turned on**.
Users can't access shared resources	When **Password Protected Sharing is turned on** people who have a user account and password on your computer can access shared resources. *If you want to give others access to your shared data but you don't want to create user accounts on your computer for them, you'll have to turn off this option.*

Create a Standard user account for yourself and only use the Administrator account in emergencies

Do you still use the account that was set up when you set up the computer? If you do, you have an Administrator account. Would you like to switch so you're not using the administrator account as your day-to-day login? Sounds good, doesn't it, but there's a problem. Although Standard user accounts provide better security and protection than Administrator accounts, you've seen how, when you create a new Standard user account, that account's completely *new*. It's not configured with a Desktop background, it doesn't contain any Desktop shortcuts, and users can't access any personal files without inputting and administrator name and password . . .

And that's the problem. If you switched, would you have to create a new account and move all of your data, recreate e-mail accounts in your e-mail program, and reconfigure your personal settings all over again?

And still more problems. What if you don't want to set up sharing or configure Libraries to allow access to your "administrator" data if you logged in as a Standard user? It's your data and if you put the data in a Public folder, all the other users would be able to see it, too. This seems like a lose–lose situation. Is there anything can you do?

You bet. You can create a new Administrator account (because all PCs have to have at least one) and then downsize your own account to Standard. You'll be able to keep all of your settings, data, network information, and everything else related to your account, but your account will be a Standard account, not an Administrator account.

Now, you can't create an account named Administrator. You just can't. But you *can* create one called Admin or Administrator2. The steps are the same as creating a Standard user account except that at step 3, you choose an Administrator account type:

1. Click Start > Control Panel > **Add or remove user accounts**.

2. Click **Create a new account**.

3. Type a name for the new user, let's call this one "Admin," click **Administrator**, and click **Create Account**.

4. Find the new Admin account in the Control Panel (click Add or remove user accounts), and complete the steps required to assign a password.

Your computer now has two Administrator accounts. Yours and the new Admin account. Now you can downsize your account to a standard user account.

5. Select your own account and opt to make changes to it. Select **Change your account type**. Work through the steps to change the account from Administrator to Standard.

Make changes to your user account

For good measure, reboot the computer. This allows you to log on with your Standard account, and will also allow you to see the new Administrator account during logon. Your account will look exactly as it did. The only changes you'll notice, initially at least, is that once logged on you'll have to input Administrator credentials when you want to make changes that will affect all users on the computer.

Note: There are a few things you'll need to be logged on as an Administrator to do, for instance to change UAC settings. If this situation ever arises, you'll have to log off your standard account and log on with Administrator credentials.

If you ever decide that your new Standard account is just too annoying—inputting an Administrator's password every time you want to make a system-wide change or install software gets old, fast—you can change everything back to the way it was. Just go into the Control Panel and change your account type back to an Administrator account.

Take a break

It's that time again. Lucky you. It's time to take a break. You may be tempted to keep forging ahead, but fight the urge. Studies show that your retention of new material will actually increase if you walk away now and then to give your learning muscles a much-deserved break. So, go take a break, if for no other reason than that the science made you do it.

Review

○ There are three account types on your Windows 7 PC. Select the correct three:

☐ Limited user   ☐ Standard

☐ Administrator   ☐ Guest

☐ Manager   ☐ Installer

○ Your mother visits several times a year and stays for two weeks. She needs access to your PC, but she also needs to be able to install her cell phone software, access her e-mail, surf the Internet, and play games. You'd like her be able to personalize her computer experience too, with screen savers and Desktop backgrounds. What type of account should you create for her, and why? Select one and add the reasons.

☐ A password-protected Administrator account is best because

....

☐ A password-protected Standard account is best because

....

☐ None, enabling the Guest account is best because

....

○ When you create a new user account you must:

→ Open .... from the Start menu.

→ Create the new account and select an account ....

→ Select the new account to apply a .... to protect the account from nosy relatives.

○ Multiple users have options when sharing a single computer:

→ The .... feature allows two or more users to be logged on at the same time, and does not require users to close programs and log off.

→ The .... feature allows a user to complete log off of the computer to free up resources for other users.

→ The .... and .... options on the Start menu let you power down the computer without turning it off completely when no one is using it.

Continues, flip the page

↻ The Guest account allows you to temporarily offer access to visitors. While using the Guest account:

→ Users can .... and
....

→ Users cannot .... or
....

↻ Parental Controls allow you to restrict a particular account, and:

→ Can only be applied to .... user accounts.

→ Can be configured to limit how much .... a user can spend logged on the computer.

→ Can be configured to control .... ratings.

→ Can be configured to control what .... a user can access and use.

↻ Sharing issues arise often but can almost always be resolved by creating a user account for the troubled user on the PC that holds the shared data. However, there are other options. If you do not want to create a user account on your PC for a user that needs access, you can:

→ Enable File and .... Sharing to ....
....

→ Enable .... Folder Sharing to ....
....

→ Enable Media .... to ....
....

→ Enable Password Protected Sharing to ....

→ Disable Password Protected Sharing to ....

↻ Why is a Standard user account inherently safer than an Administrator account?

....
....
....

How did you do?

Did you forget anything? It's hard to remember it all. Go ahead and re-read the sections covering what you overlooked. Your brain might need a bit more time to absorb all the information.

Experiment

The best way to really cement these features and techniques into your long-term memory is to expand on the techniques you just learned about by using them and taking them just one step further.

Here are some suggestions for your experiment using techniques covered in this chapter.

Create a password reset disk

Now that you have passwords, can you imagine the trouble you'd be in if you forgot the Administrator password or your own password?

You should never have to imagine. There's an easy way to create a password reset disk. Should you ever forget your password you can use this disk to create a new password.

To get started, insert some kind of disk (CDR (writable CD), flash, media card), and then navigate to the Control Panel's User Accounts and Family Safety, and click **User Accounts**. There, click **Create a password reset disk**.

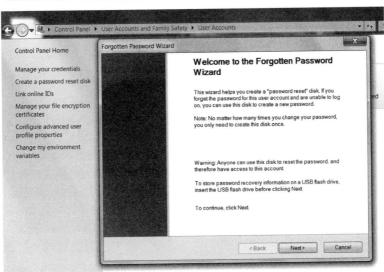

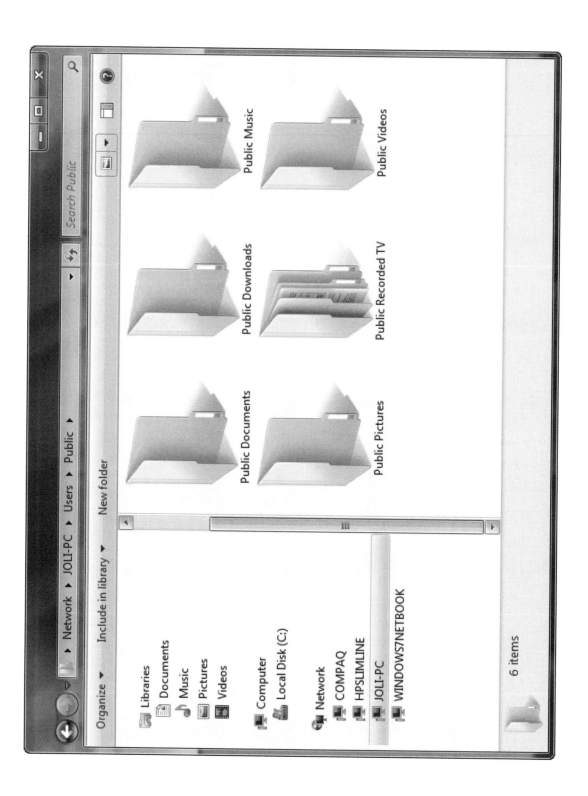

11 Share data over a mixed network

You have all kinds of PCs. One runs XP, two run Vista, and one runs Windows 7. And sharing over what's called a "mixed network" can throw up a few issues.

⇨ Are there copies of your latest vacation pictures on more than one computer?

⇨ Do you e-mail data you need to share with others on your network instead of creating a folder specifically for data you'd like to pass back and forth?

⇨ If you have multiple copies of music and other media on your network, is browsing through duplicate copies to find want you want annoying? And what about those duplicate (or triplicate) titles in Windows Media Center, Media Player, and iTunes—wouldn't it be great if you could delete those?

⇨ Is there a communal printer you can't access?

Networks are supposed to make it *easier* to share data, not harder . . .

No Problem!

You can share all kinds of data over any type of network with computers running various editions of operating systems. You can easily enable:

⇨ File and Printer Sharing

⇨ Public Folder Sharing

⇨ Media Sharing on your Windows 7 PC and others, and share everything you want effortlessly

And you can configure user accounts (chapter 10) to secure it all. You can even share your personal folders, or, folders you create anywhere on your PC.

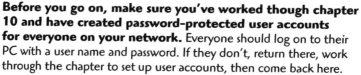

Stop!
Before you go on, make sure you've worked though chapter 10 and have created password-protected user accounts for everyone on your network. Everyone should log on to their PC with a user name and password. If they don't, return there, work through the chapter to set up user accounts, then come back here.

Share data with everyone on the network with Public Folder Sharing

You want to resolve your sharing problems fast. You don't care about protocols, permissions, or access controls; you don't care about mixed networks; you just want the no-hassle version of sharing. Well, here it is.

Move (or copy or save) what you want to share to the Public folders on your PC and enable **Public Folder Sharing**.

How does that work? Is it really that simple? Yes. When you put data in the Public folders, and when Public Folder Sharing is enabled, anyone on your network can access that data. It's **Public**. No muss; no fuss. If you want to add a bit more security into the mix, enable password-protected sharing. That way users will have to enter a valid user name and password to access the data.

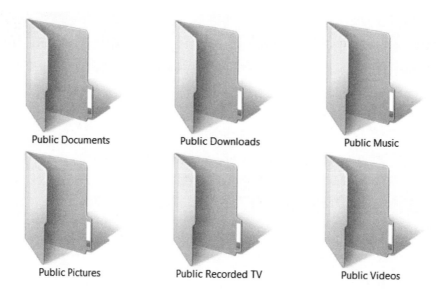

Public Documents   Public Downloads   Public Music

Public Pictures   Public Recorded TV   Public Videos

Public folders are part of the Windows 7 file system and are already created for you.

It's easy three-step process to share data using the Public folders:

1. Enable the **sharing options** you prefer.

2. **Move**, **copy**, or **save the data** you want to share to any of the **Public folders**. (Quickfire question: why is moving data better than having a copy of the same data on two computers?)

3. Create a shortcut to the Public folders on your Desktop or access them via your Libraries.

> **Note:** This chapter is about **mixed networks**. If your network only contains Windows 7 PCs, refer to chapter 12 to learn how to create a HomeGroup. A HomeGroup can only be created among Windows 7 PCs, but it makes sharing much easier, because it automatically enables the proper sharing settings when it's set up. You can combine sharing methods as desired, though; for instance, you can create a HomeGroup between two Windows 7 PCs while manually sharing or using Public folders for sharing with non-Windows 7 PCs.

1. Turn on Public Folder Sharing

First you need to enable Public Folder Sharing. It's easy:

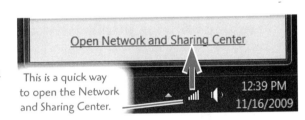

1. Click the network icon on the Taskbar in the Notification area and click **Open Network and Sharing Center**.

    This is a quick way to open the Network and Sharing Center.

2. In the Network and Sharing Center, click **Change advanced sharing settings**. This option is in the Tasks pane on the left side.

    Change advanced sharing settings

3. Scroll down to **Public folder sharing**, and click **Turn on sharing so anyone with network access can read and write files in the Public folder**. To require a password, scroll down some more and under Password protected sharing, click **Turn on password protected sharing**.

Public folder sharing

When Public folder sharing is on, people on the network, including homegroup members, can access files in the Public folders. <u>What are the Public folders?</u>

⊙ Turn on sharing so anyone with network access can read and write files in the Public folders

4. Click Save Changes.

2. Move (or copy) data to Public folders

Now what? Now you simply save new data, or move or copy existing data to the appropriate Public folders. While there are lots of ways to do this, it's easiest to position two windows on your screen, one with the Public folder open and one with your personal folder open, and then just drag and drop data as desired:

1. First, click the folder icon on the Taskbar to open your personal folder. Drag the folder's menu bar to the top left side of the screen so it "snaps" into place.

2. Next, click Start, click Computer, and drill down to C:\Users\Public. Drag this window's menu bar to the top right side of the screen and let it "snap" into place.

3. Finally, locate the data in your personal folders to share (in the folder on the left of the screen), and drag that data to the appropriate Public folder on the right of the screen.

    Once you're finished, your Public folders will be populated with data others on your network can access.

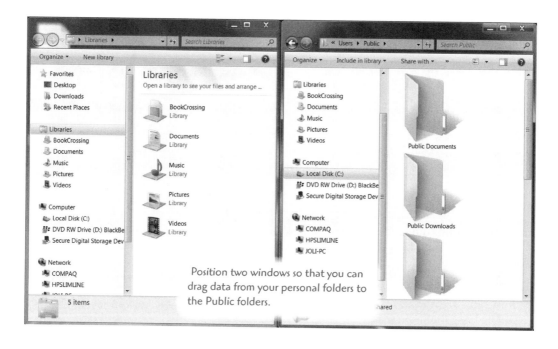

Position two windows so that you can drag data from your personal folders to the Public folders.

Note: There are a few things to know about moving or copying folders to Public folders:

▶ *If you drag a Library to the Public folders, a* **shortcut** *is created to that Library in the Public folder.* When you access the Public folder on your PC, you can use the shortcut to access the Library and all the items in it. Network users won't be able to access the Library via the shortcut, though, unless you *also* share the Library, allowing access to everything in it. You'll learn how to share a Library shortly.

▶ *If you drag a folder from your* **personal folder** *to a* **Public library**, *the data is* **moved**. It will no longer appear in your personal library, and will only be available in your Public Library. This is the best option for data you *know* you want to share, because it reduces the duplication you'll see if you opt to copy the data.

▶ If you'd rather copy data than move it, hold down the **right mouse key** to drag a folder (you use the left mouse key to drag usually) if you want the option to **copy** the data or to **move** it.

3. Access the Public folders from your personal folder

Where are the Public folders? Sure they're under C:\, under Users, and under Public, but getting there's a lot of work, right? It's OK; you can find the Public folders inside your personal folder.

Here, you can see the list of Libraries, with Pictures expanded. What do you remember about the locations the Pictures Library accesses by default?

Right, the Pictures Library offers access to My Pictures and Public Pictures by default. Other Public folders work the same way, accessing both your folders and the corresponding Public folders by default.

This Public Pictures folder has subfolders that have either been moved or copied there.

Play with it

In order to use Public folders regularly, you must be able to get to them quickly. You need to know how to find the Public folders from your personal folder. You also need to find out what's currently in those folders; maybe other users who access your computer have put stuff there! Finally, after seeing how easy it is to browse to the Public folders, you may decide to move the data you want to share there instead of copying it or sharing other folders manually, so you'll need easy access to the Public folders.

To access the folders quickly, to see what's in them, and to again consider what you can move there to share with others:

1. Click Start, then click your user name at the top of the Start menu.

2. Under Libraries, expand Documents and click **Public Documents**; expand **Music** and click **Public Music**; expand **Pictures** and click **Public Pictures**, and expand **Videos** and click **Public Videos**. What do you see in each? Has anyone else put data there? Write down what you see here:

Public Documents: ....

Public Music: ....

Public Pictures: ....

Public Videos: ....

What data could you move there? Have you considered moving data from other PCs here to consolidate your data? Maybe you could copy backups here?

Create a shortcut to the Public folders for easy access

Once you've committed to using Public folders, it's a pain to expand each of the libraries and navigate through to access the Public folder. If you use the Public folders every day, wouldn't it be great if there was a way to make the Public folders much easier to access?

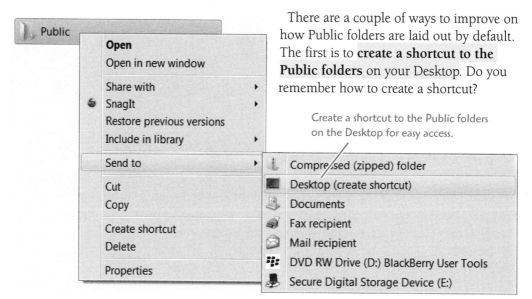

There are a couple of ways to improve on how Public folders are laid out by default. The first is to **create a shortcut to the Public folders** on your Desktop. Do you remember how to create a shortcut?

Create a shortcut to the Public folders on the Desktop for easy access.

Now you can use the shortcut to access the Public folder directly from the Desktop or from any window that offers access to the Desktop folders.

The second way to configure better access to the Public folders is to create a new library and include the Public folder in it. But wait, does that sound kind of complicated to you?

Once a shortcut is created you can access the Public folder from almost anywhere.

Create a Public Library

There's no Public Library by default, but you can **create a Public Library and include the C:\Users\Public folders in it for easy access**. Do you remember how to create Libraries? If you don't remember how to do it, return to chapter 9 for a refresher. Create a new Library called Public, and include the Public folders in it.

Once you're finished, your personal folder should include something like this:

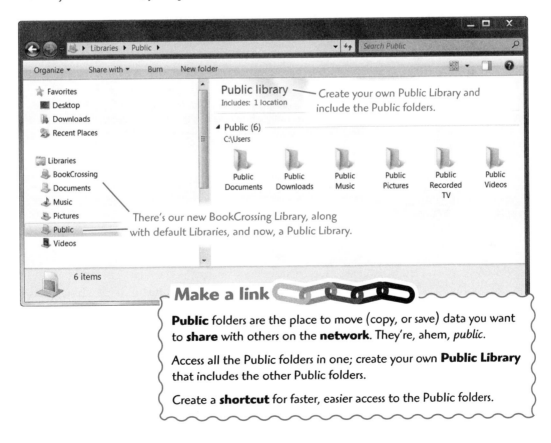

Create your own Public Library and include the Public folders.

There's our new BookCrossing Library, along with default Libraries, and now, a Public Library.

Make a link

Public folders are the place to move (copy, or save) data you want to **share** with others on the **network**. They're, ahem, *public*.

Access all the Public folders in one; create your own **Public Library** that includes the other Public folders.

Create a **shortcut** for faster, easier access to the Public folders.

Share files and printers, fast

You've shared files and you've shared printers on your Windows 7 PC, but network users still can't access them. What gives?

You need to turn on File and Printer Sharing. The steps to do that are the same as the steps for turning on Public Folder sharing. Look for advanced sharing in the Network and Sharing Center.

Sharing option	What it means
Turn on **File and Printer Sharing and** turn off **password-protected sharing**	**ALL files and printers you have shared can be accessed** by users on the network.
Turn on **File and Printer Sharing and** enable **password-protected sharing**	Only people who have a user account and password **on your computer can access shared files and printers** attached to your computer, and to the Public folders.

You'll have to decide what you'd prefer before moving forward.

Warning
Anyone on the network includes visitors who use your computers, your mother-in-law who's supposed to be taking a nap, and the cleaning lady who comes in while you're at work. For these reasons it's often best to enable password-protected sharing, and work through the required steps (outlined in chapter 10) to create user accounts for those who need access.

Share a folder, Library, or other area on your hard drive

Public folders and sharing music, photos, and videos is fine . . . at first. The problem is that you've hit a few snags. **Not all data that needs to be shared needs to be shared with** *everyone.*

→ What if you want to share information with only *some* of the users who have user accounts on your computer?

→ And is it is possible to share information with *some* but not *all* of the users who have network access to your Public folders with no need for passwords and user accounts?

You can't put data in a Public folder and share it with only certain people. Public means public, even if you do make people type a user name and password. Can you get around this somehow?

To specify who can view the data (and exclude anyone not on the list) you need to **manually share data** and specifically state who can access it. You can manually share just about anything, from a single folder, Library, or hard disk drive (although the latter isn't recommended) to a CD/DVD drive, printer, or external hard drive.

Decide what you need to share *over a mixed network* then:

1. Right-click the item to share.

2. Click **Share with > Specific people...** .

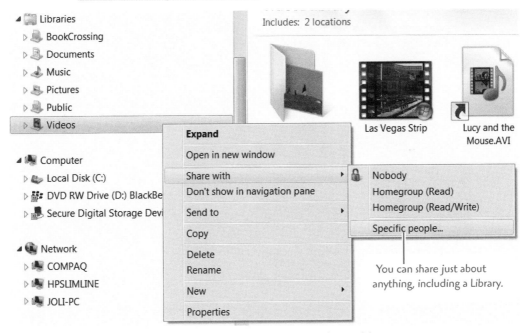

You can share just about anything, including a Library.

3. Click the arrow to select the people you want to let access your shared data. Click **Add**.

Choose people to share with

Type a name and then click Add, or click the arrow to find someone.

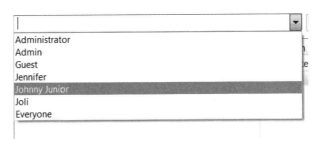

4. The new user(s) will appear in the list, where you can assign different permission levels.

Choose people to share with

Type a name and then click Add, or click the arrow to find someone.

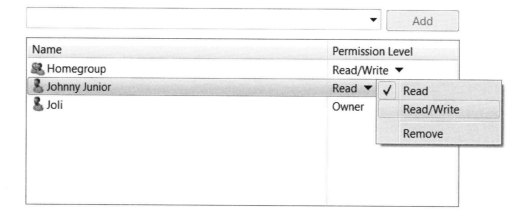

5. When you've added the specific people and set their permission levels, click **Share**. You may be prompted to give other people access to similar folders and Libraries. To allow access to these additional folders, click Next.

- -

Take a break

Your brain needs time to sift through what you just learned about sharing over a mixed network. Time to take a break. We're nearly at the end of the chapter. All that's left is an Experiment or two. So, walk away. Give yourself this opportunity to digest all that we've covered. This is a perfect time for a cup of tea or flipping through a magazine. Afterward, come back to see what you can recall and then experiment with your new Sharing skills.

Review

↻ Public folders are a place to move, copy, or save data to share with others on your network. To use Public folders as a sharing option you have to enable .... sharing in the Network and Sharing .... You can open the Network and Sharing Center from the Taskbar's .... area.

↻ To require each user to input a user name and password prior to accessing data in the Public folders, you must create a user account for them on your PC and then enable .... Sharing.

↻ There are six Public folders: Documents, ..., ..., ..., Recorded TV, and ....

↻ When moving or copying data to the Public folders the following statements are true:

☐ If you drag a Library to the Public folders, a shortcut is created to that Library the in the Public folder.

☐ Network users can access the all of the data in your Library via the shortcut, even if you don't specifically share the Library.

☐ Left-click and drag to move data.

☐ Right-click and drag to copy data.

☐ It's okay to copy data; you won't have a problem with duplicates showing up in Media Player or Media Center.

☐ Public folders are located in C:\Public.

↻ From the Network and Sharing Center's Advanced Sharing Options you can turn on or off Network ...., File and .... Sharing, Public .... Sharing, Media Streaming, File Sharing Connections, ..., and HomeGroup Connections.

Continues, flip the page

↺ To share a folder manually instead of moving or copying data to a Public folder:

1. Browse to the folder to share and ....-........................ it.

2. Click Share with ....

3. Click the arrow to select users and then click ....

4. Click the arrow to assign .... that include Read, .../............................., Remove.

5. Click Share.

How did you do?

Did you forget anything? It's hard to remember it all. Go ahead and re-read the sections covering what you overlooked. Your brain might need a bit more time to absorb all the information.

Experiment

The best way to really cement these features and techniques into your long-term memory is to expand on the techniques you just learned about by using them and taking them just one step further.

Here are some suggestions for your experiment using techniques covered in this chapter.

Share files outside of your network

Do you ever need to share files with people who are not on or cannot access your network? For instance, do you want to be able to work on large files at home and let your boss access them at work, without having to e-mail them or post them to an FTP site? If so, go to **Office Live Workspace** (`http://workspace.officelive.com`) and create an online workspace where you can share data with others for free.

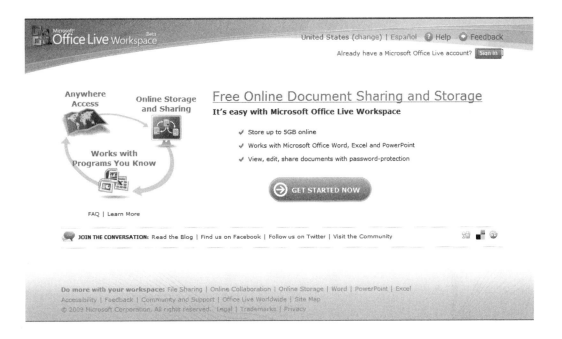

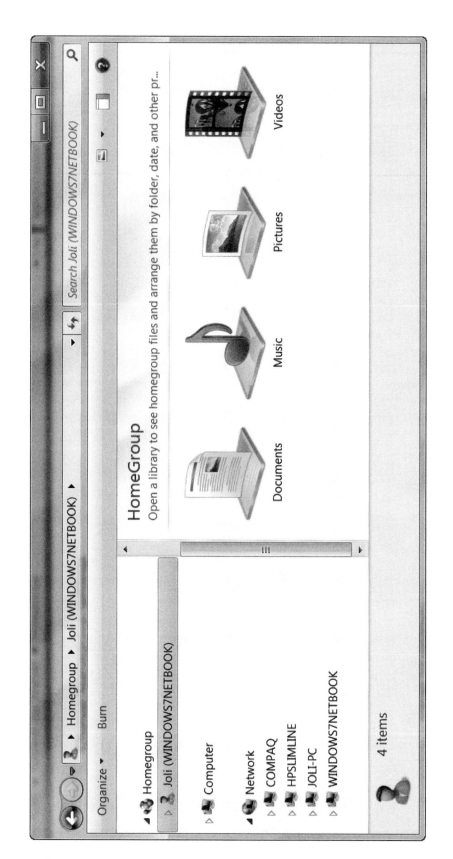

12 Create a Windows 7 HomeGroup

You know how to share data using Public folders with everyone on your network, how to create user accounts, and how to share personal folders, printers, and even the disc drives connected to your PC, but it's a pain:

⇨ Should you opt for password-protected sharing?

⇨ What data does File and Printer Sharing really share and with whom?

⇨ What permissions should you apply?

⇨ Which users should you allow?

⇨ Do you really want *any* of your personal data in Public folders?

⇨ Why does sharing seem to be so difficult?

Is there an easier way?

No Problem!

An easier way to share has arrived, but it only works when you're sharing data with another Windows 7 PC (or multiple Windows 7 PCs) on your home network. To use this new sharing feature, you create a HomeGroup. With a HomeGroup, you can easily share music, photos, videos, and even documents, and Windows will configure the proper sharing settings for you. You can even stream media to devices that are Windows 7 compatible, share printers, and set permissions. If you have two or more Windows 7 PCs, read on. If you don't, you'll have to set up sharing as detailed in chapter 11.

What's a HomeGroup?

Do you remember the first time you turned on the PC running Windows 7? If Windows 7 found a network, you were prompted to choose Home, Work, or Public. You may also have been prompted to create (or join) a HomeGroup.

You probably remember the network stuff since that's what you've been using to connect to the Internet, but what's a **HomeGroup**? It's a new way of sharing files (music, photos, videos and documents) with other Windows 7 machines on your home network. It's a simple way to share data among a *group* of computers in your *home*.

You need to see what type of network you have and whether you've set up a HomeGroup, find the HomeGroup password if applicable, and see how the HomeGroup is configured. If there's no HomeGroup, you'll need to create one. (You can't create a HomeGroup in Windows 7 Home Basic or Starter, but you can join one.)

> **Warning**
> Before you continue, it's best to create user accounts for everyone who you want to allow access to data on your computer as detailed in chapter 10. While there are ways around this, creating user accounts increases security and makes everything work like it's supposed to without any special tweaking or configuration.

Find out if you have a HomeGroup, and, if not, create or join one

1. Click the network icon in the Notification area of the Taskbar and click **Open Network and Sharing Center**.

2. Look for HomeGroup. If it reads:

   a. **Ready to create**, you do not yet have a HomeGroup and can create one.

   b. **Available to join**, a HomeGroup has been created on another Windows 7 PC on your network and you can join it.

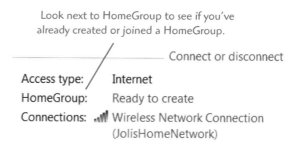

Look next to HomeGroup to see if you've already created or joined a HomeGroup.

Connect or disconnect

Access type: Internet
HomeGroup: Ready to create
Connections: Wireless Network Connection (JolisHomeNetwork)

   c. **Joined**, you are already part of a HomeGroup or have already created one.

What if you don't see HomeGroup listed at all? That means your network type is configured as either Work or Public. Click the network type (here it's a Work network) to change the network type to **Home**. When you're done, continue with the steps below to create your HomeGroup.

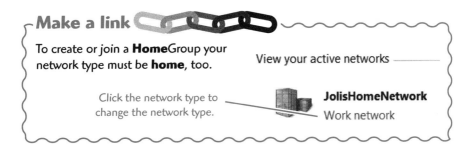

Make a link

To create or join a **Home**Group your network type must be **home**, too.

View your active networks

Click the network type to change the network type.

JolisHomeNetwork
Work network

Create a HomeGroup

1. In the Network and Sharing Center, click **Ready to Create**. (Remember, the network type must be set to **Home**.)

2. Read the information about HomeGroups, then click **Create a HomeGroup**.

3. **Choose the Libraries you want to share.** Do you remember what your Libraries contain? Don't worry; users will have to enter an account name and password to gain access to your shared data. And later, you'll learn how to exclude certain folders or change these settings if desired.

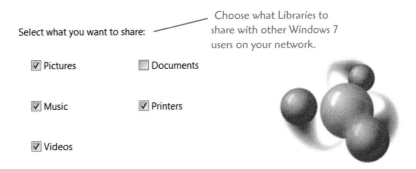

Select what you want to share:

Choose what Libraries to share with other Windows 7 users on your network.

☑ Pictures   ☐ Documents

☑ Music   ☑ Printers

☑ Videos

4. Write down the password you just created and keep it somewhere safe, but not near your computer.

Now you can add other Windows 7 PCs to your new HomeGroup. You'll need to join the HomeGroup from each those PCs.

Join a HomeGroup

1. Open the Network and Sharing Center, and next to HomeGroup, click **Available to join**.

2. Read the information about HomeGroups, then click **Join now**.

3. Select the Libraries on *this* PC that you want to share, and click Next.

4. Type in your HomeGroup's password. Capital letters count!

Access type: Internet
HomeGroup: Available to join
Connections: .ıll Wireless Network Connection (JolisHomeNetwork)

> Uh oh. Did you forget to write down the password? Go back to the first PC, the one you created the HomeGroup on initially, open the Network and Sharing Center, and, next to HomeGroup, click Joined. You can access View or print the HomeGroup password from there.

Play with it

HomeGroup permissions

Now that you have at least two Windows 7 PCs configured in a HomeGroup you can open shared data with Windows Explorer and edit it. On one of the PCs, open your personal folder. Note the new item in the Navigation pane and the list of HomeGroup computers.

Do you see other computers that are part of the HomeGroup?

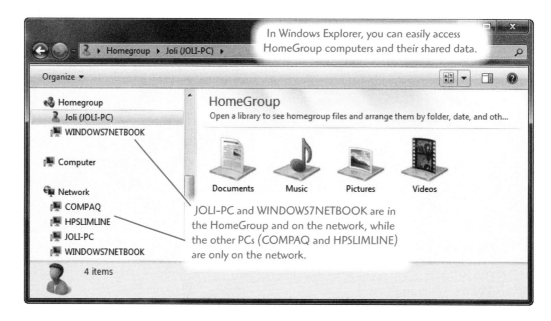

Select any HomeGroup computer, then locate and open a document that's been shared. Type a few new words in the document and click Save.

What folder does the edited document try to save to?

....

Is the default folder on your computer or the originating one?

....

What happens if you browse to the original location of the file and try to save changes there (in essence to write over the original file in the original location)?

....

What permissions do you think Windows 7 grants by default when a HomeGroup is created?

....

When you create a HomeGroup and share Libraries, by default, other HomeGroup users only have Read access. That means when a user on another networked HomeGroup PC accesses a document you've created, they can open and read it. So far so good, that's part of sharing. But the other user can't write over your document. Of course, users *can* open and access your data, *make changes*, and then save *their* changes with another filename on their PC or to a Public folder; that's part of sharing too.

Can you see any problems with all your data being publicly available to everyone on your HomeGroup like this, even if you leave the default Read-only access in place?

And what if you want other users to be able to read *and* work with your files, make changes, and save the changes in the same document? After all, saving a copy of the same document is duplication and that was one of the reasons for sharing files in the first place.

The default Read access can be changed to Read/Write in the File Sharing dialog.

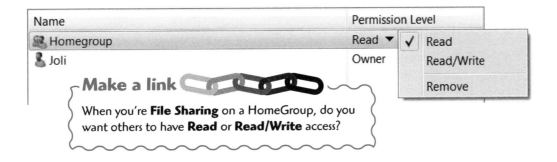

Make a link

When you're **File Sharing** on a HomeGroup, do you want others to have **Read** or **Read/Write** access?

HomeGroup benefits and personalization

Now that you've created a HomeGroup you can access data on HomeGroup computers without the previous hassles related to sharing and accessing shared data. For instance, if you shared your Documents Library, you, as well as other HomeGroup users with user accounts on your PC, can access your documents from another PC. The same is true of music, pictures, and videos.

If you want to stream pictures, music, and video to all devices on the network, including an Xbox or other media extender (which is different from simply sharing data with users), you'll need to enable **Stream media with devices** in the HomeGroup settings.

> **Warning**
> When you opt to stream media, it's important to understand that the shared media *isn't secure*. Anyone that's connected to your network can access the shared media and receive it. This makes sense, because devices aren't generally capable of inputting user names and passwords, and you want your media extender to be capable of playing your media!

If you worked through chapters 5 and 6, and have already enabled media streaming, you're good to go. You can easily access shared music from inside programs, including Media Player. You'll find the music shared under Other Libraries in the sidebar.

After creating a HomeGroup and opting to share music, you can access the music easily in Media Player.

The Windows 7 Netbook contains all of the music shown. The music on this PC in the HomeGroup is accessible from Other Libraries on any other PC in the HomeGroup.

Play with it

Open Media Player, and locate **Other Libraries**. You may see PCs that aren't in the HomeGroup, but you're looking for a PC that's in the HomeGroup. Select the HomeGroup PC, then click Music, Videos, Pictures, Recorded TV and/or Playlists. To play any media, simply click it.

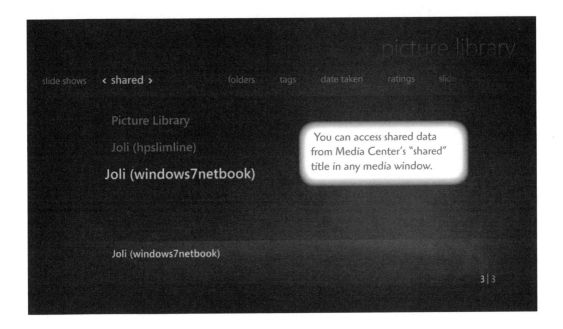

If you can't stream music, check if streaming is enabled. Open the **Network and Sharing Center**, click **Choose HomeGroup** and sharing options. Place a check in the appropriate box or review the current media sharing settings.

Share media with devices

☑ Stream my pictures, music, and videos to all devices on my home network

Choose media streaming options...

Note: Shared media is not secure. Anyone connected to your network can receive your shared media.

If you only have one PC with a TV tuner, you can record TV on that PC and access it from another with media streaming and sharing enabled.

You can access recorded TV from Media Player and Media Center. Again, refer to chapters 5 and 6 for more information on using and sharing media.

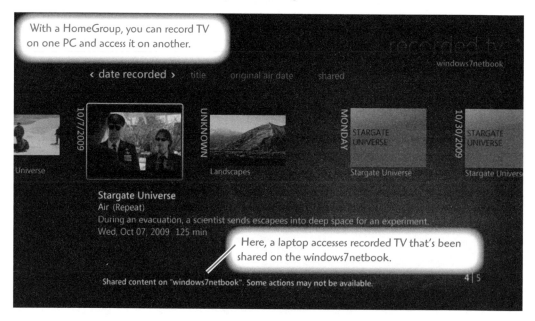

Of course, you can access pictures, videos, and documents, too, by browsing to them in their respective folders. But remember, there are two types of sharing permissions, Read and Read/Write. By default, you can only "read" shared data. You'll need Read/Write permission to write over existing data belonging to someone else.

Keep specific files and folders from being shared

Sharing information via a HomeGroup is nice, but what if you *don't* want to share everything in your Pictures Library? What if you want to exclude a few folders right away before anyone sees what's in them?

No problem; it's easy. To exclude any folder and to keep it from being shared with others:

1. Browse to the folder.

2. Right-click the folder you want to exclude from the shared files.

3. Click **Share with > Nobody**.

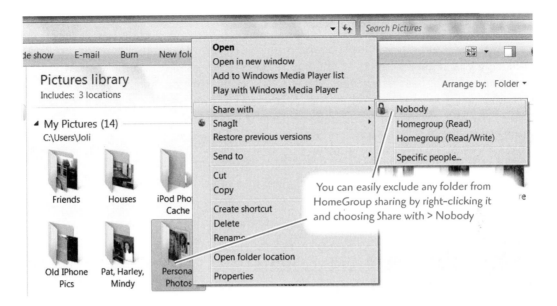

You can easily exclude any folder from HomeGroup sharing by right-clicking it and choosing Share with > Nobody

Share personal folders and other Libraries

That's excluding settled, but what about *including* folders that aren't shared by default in any of the Libraries that are? To include any folder to share it with others:

1. Browse to the folder.

2. Right-click the folder you want to share.

3. Click **Share with** > **HomeGroup (Read)** or **HomeGroup (Read/write)**. Remember, if you choose **Read**, users can *access* but **not** *change* the data. If you choose **Read/write**, users can *access* and *edit* the data.

Are you still having some sharing issues, even after setting up a HomeGroup? Are there any things that bug you about your HomeGroup? Things like:

→ What if you don't want to create a Windows account for everyone you want to allow to access files on your computer?

→ Can you share certain documents with some people on your network but not with others without creating user accounts for everyone?

→ Or maybe other users on your network don't want to create an account for you on their PCs. If you just can't convince them that it really doesn't take up much hard drive space at all, and is very secure, is there any other way to share data?

Link on online ID with a user account

The best way resolve these issues is to link your online ID with your user account. **Linking your online ID** with your user account only works on a HomeGroup, but once you've linked an online ID, you can use that ID to access your information on other computers, including one in another location (like work or home) without having a user account there. Other network users can use your online ID to allow you to access shared files on their PC instead of creating a user account too, and you can do the same with others' online IDs.

What is an online ID though? Right now it's a Windows Live ID, like an e-mail address ending in .Live or .Hotmail. Did you get a Windows Live ID back in chapter 2? If you didn't, now may be the time to reconsider.

Once you have a Windows Live ID, you can link it with your user account and reap the benefits! It's a lengthy process, but you'll only need to do it once and it's definitely worth it.

1. In the Start Search window type **Link ID**.

2. From the results click **Link online IDs**.

3. Click **Add an online ID provider**.

4. Download and install the Windows Live ID Sign-in Assistant. (There are quite a few steps involved here, but mostly they involve clicking Run, Run again, accepting terms of service, installing, and rebooting the PC.)

5. After rebooting the PC, return to the Link IDs page and click **Link online ID**.

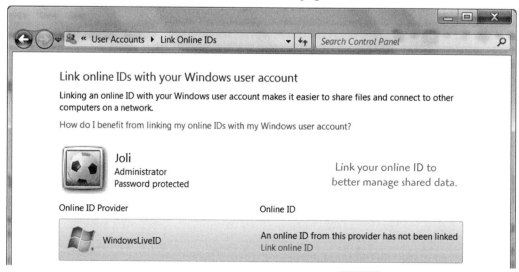

6. Type your Windows Live ID and password, and click **Sign in**.

7. Click OK.

Play with it

Now here's the fun part. Let's say your co-worker has linked her online ID with her user name on her netbook. You've just linked your online user ID with your PC. You have a folder named Business Plans that you want to share with your colleague, but not with everyone in the HomeGroup. So how do you change who sees what?

Just remove the HomeGroup from the list of people to share with, and add her online ID. She's the only one in the HomeGroup that now has access.

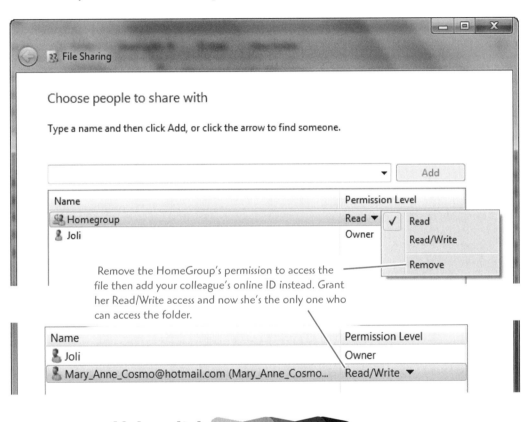

Remove the HomeGroup's permission to access the file then add your colleague's online ID instead. Grant her Read/Write access and now she's the only one who can access the folder.

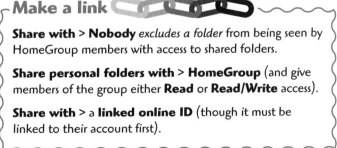

Make a link

Share with > Nobody *excludes a folder* from being seen by HomeGroup members with access to shared folders.

Share personal folders with > HomeGroup (and give members of the group either **Read** or **Read/Write** access).

Share with > a linked online ID (though it must be linked to their account first).

Network and sharing fixes

Sometimes, the problems you run into with sharing and accessing shared data don't have anything at all to do with the way you've shared the data. It doesn't have to do with permissions or HomeGroup settings, and there's no built-in bug in the Public folders. Sometimes, something just goes haywire with the network. If you receive a "network error," don't second guess yourself; consider that it may be a network issue.

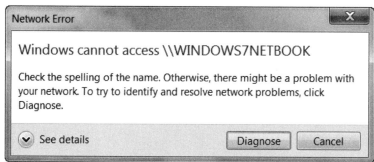

You may not have done anything wrong to get a network error. Did the user rename their computer? Is it turned on? Is it connected to the network?

To resolve networking problems there are several things to try:

1. Make sure the computer you're trying to access is turned on and connected to the network.

2. Check that Ethernet cables are securely inserted, that wireless hardware is turned on, and that the computer is close enough to the wireless access point to send and receive data, if applicable.

3. Click **Diagnose** when an error message appears. Almost always, performing the first solution will resolve networking problems.

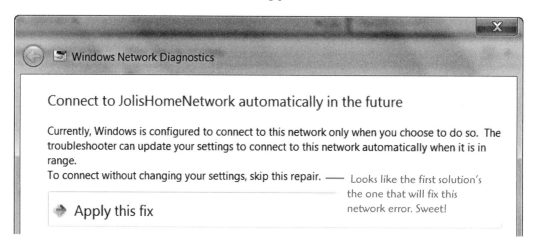

Looks like the first solution's the one that will fix this network error. Sweet!

4. Open the Network and Sharing Center and check the **Network Map**. If you can't see the networked computer there, *it* isn't connected. If you don't see any networked computers, *you* aren't connected!

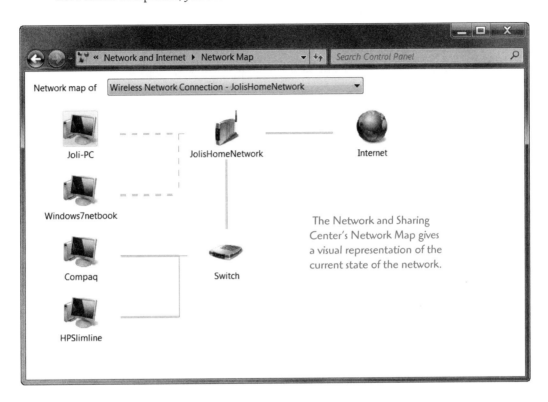

The Network and Sharing Center's Network Map gives a visual representation of the current state of the network.

Take a break

It's time to take a break. Take some time, walk away and give your brain some much needed time away from learning new things. This is a great time to go for a walk or catch up with that pile of mail sitting on the corner of your desk. When you're ready, come back for the Review and Experiment to test your newly learned skills.

Review

○ There are three types of networks: ...., ..., and .... To create a HomeGroup the network type must be configured as ....

○ One way to access the Network and Sharing Center to create or join a HomeGroup is from the Taskbar's .... area. Just click

....

○ In the Network and Sharing Center, there are several HomeGroup options:

Ready to create means ....

....

Available to join means ....

....

.... means you're already part of a HomeGroup.

○ If you don't see a HomeGroup option in the Network and Sharing

Center, it's because ....

To resolve this issue you must ....

....

....

....

○ Where can you locate the HomeGroup password if you forget it?

....

....

....

○ There are two kinds of permissions that can be applied to HomeGroup shares. One is Read, and the other is Read/Write. Which is set by default when a new HomeGroup is created?

....

↺ What's the easiest way to exclude a folder that's part of a shared Library in a HomeGroup?

☐ Move the folder out of the Library and to a part of the hard drive that isn't monitored by the HomeGroup, and apply permissions manually.

☐ Right-click the folder, remove the HomeGroup, and add the users you want to give access.

☐ Right-click the folder and choose Private.

☐ Drag the folder to the Desktop where it won't be monitored, link a user ID on all of the other networked PCs, and then add the linked ID as a user.

↺ How can you get around having to create user accounts on your PC for everyone who needs access to the data on it? For instance, how can you allow a person on your network access to one folder on your PC, without having to create a user account?

....

....

....

↺ When you receive a network error message you should click .... and see if Windows can resolve the problem automatically or offer a solution for you to try.

How did you do?

Did you forget anything? It's hard to remember it all. Go ahead and re-read the sections covering what you overlooked. Your brain might need a bit more time to absorb all the information.

Take some time to re-read your links, or if you didn't remember them, consider creating a new link that's bigger, sillier, scarier, more extreme; anything to make it more memorable.

Experiment

The best way to really cement these features and techniques into your long-term memory is to expand on the techniques you just learned about by using them and taking them just one step further.

Here are some suggestions for your experiment using techniques covered in this chapter.

Get rid of unnecessary user accounts

If you prefer to link to an online user ID, and you've created user accounts for people that no longer require access to your PC, you can remove them. You may also want to remove user accounts for people who only need access to a single folder on your PC, and replace that account with a linked, online ID.

To get started, click Control Panel > **Add or Remove User Accounts**.

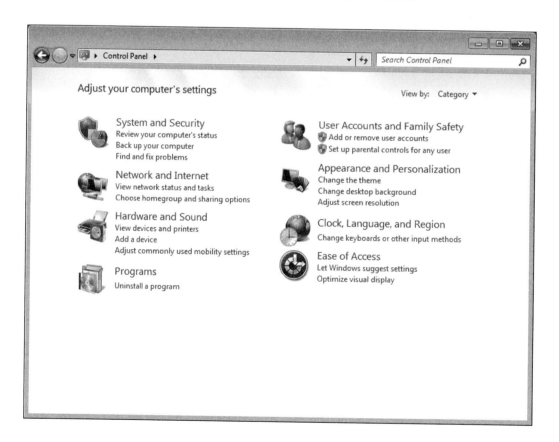

Create a folder for sharing with one person

If you have data you want to share with *only one person* on your network, you can't put that data in the Public folders; everyone would be able to see it. You can enable a HomeGroup though, and then configure the permissions (removing HomeGroup and adding the user), as detailed in this chapter. Or you could create a brand new folder anywhere on your hard drive, and share just that folder with the user.

The latter is a good option if you want to share some personal data with a temporary user to your network, like a temporary worker or visiting relative, or to share data related to a short project.

Create this type of folder now and share it with another HomeGroup user who has a linked online ID.

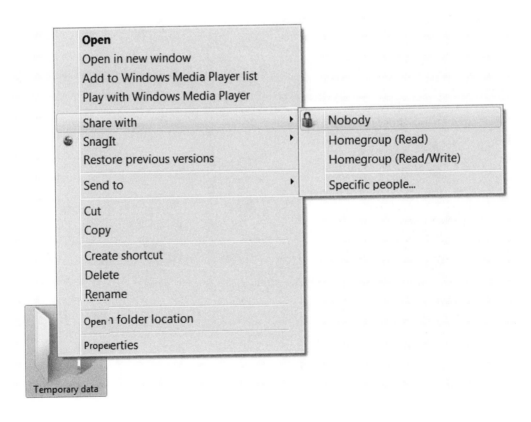

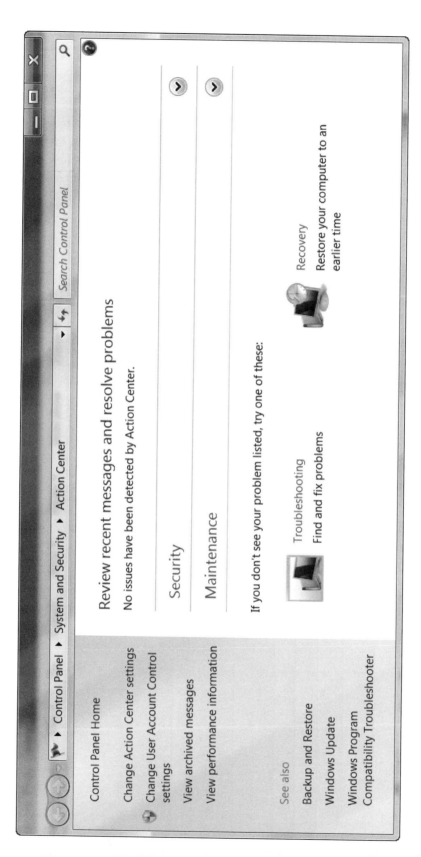

13 Keep your PC in shape

Computers slow down over time. They get bogged down with applications, slowed down by anti-virus scans, covered up with Internet Explorer toolbars and add-ons, mired in automatic updates, and cluttered with data you don't need. But you want it to be different this time. You want to deal with errors as they arise, stay safe online and away from viruses, malware, and phishing websites, and maintain your computer like an expert. You want to be able to trust your backups, and have backups for your backups! This time, you want your new Windows 7 computer to run well, and run well for a long time.

No Problem!

There are plenty of ways to ensure your computer will remain in tip-top shape. You can:

⇨ Protect yourself while online with Internet Explorer's safety features.

⇨ Understand warnings from Windows 7 and resolve them.

⇨ Use built-in tools to scan for spyware or malware.

⇨ Use the Advanced Tools to learn more about your computer and its performance.

⇨ Perform regular maintenance to prevent problems from occurring.

⇨ Back up your data regularly.

⇨ Know your Windows Experience Index and learn what you can do to improve performance.

Stay safe online

You do the best you can to stay safe while you're online, but are you still afraid of being tricked by official-looking pop-ups, entering personal information into a web page (perhaps one that looks like your bank's website but really isn't), or even having your online activities tracked without your knowledge? Although there's no foolproof solution, Internet Explorer comes with several safeguards.

You already know quite a bit about Internet Explorer. You know from previous versions that you can click Tools and Internet options to set your security level, privacy settings, delete your browsing history, and even enable the Content Advisor. Nothing's changed there but Internet Explorer has introduced some new safety features, including:

→ InPrivate Browsing

→ SmartScreen Filter

→ Pop-up Blocker settings

Prevent Internet Explorer from storing data about browsing sessions

Have your kids ever gotten on your computer, looked at your browsing history, cookies, temporary Internet files and other data for the sole purpose of uncovering what you bought them for their birthday? Do you use the public computers at an Internet café or library? Do you want to hide where you've been while in a particular browsing session? You need to enable InPrivate Browsing.

An **InPrivate Browsing** session tells Internet Explorer not to keep any record of the websites you've visited in its history, not to save cookies or keep temporary Internet files, nor save any other data. When you close the session, there will be no record of it on your PC.

To start an InPrivate session, click **Safety > InPrivate Browsing**. A new tab will open with an InPrivate icon in the address bar. That will remain until you close that tab.

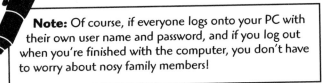

Note: Of course, if everyone logs onto your PC with their own user name and password, and if you log out when you're finished with the computer, you don't have to worry about nosy family members!

Internet Explorer reports a site's unsafe

Have you ever visited a website only for Internet Explorer to tell you the page was unsafe? That's because people who have visited the site in the past marked it as unsafe and reported it. Most often these websites are suspected of being unsafe because of activities related to "phishing," the act of trying to get personal information, credit card information, and bank account numbers from unsuspecting visitors, although they can contain other threats.

The feature that offers information about a page is called **SmartScreen Filter**. By default, it's turned on and will alert you if you visit a site that is considered unsafe. You can access the SmartScreen Filter from the **Safety** button. There you can check a current website, turn off the filter, or even report an unsafe site.

Change the Pop-up blocker settings

When you visit some websites they try to open small windows that contain ads on your computer. These small windows are called pop-ups. By default Internet Explorer blocks such pop-ups when the site tries to open them and offers a message telling you so (on its Information Bar at the top of the window, just under the tabs).

Click the message to temporarily allow pop-ups, always allow pop-ups from this site, or change the settings. There's nothing new here from previous versions, but you may not know that you can tweak the settings for this features just a little.

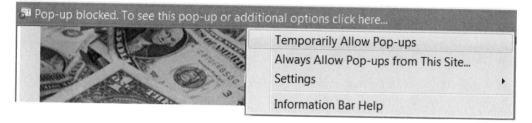

To see what you *can* change:

1. Click **Tools > Pop-up Blocker**.

2. Choose **Pop-up Blocker Settings**.

3. You can add the addresses of websites whose pop-ups you'd like to allow, but also note that you can change the Blocking Level. Make the desired changes and click OK.

Make a link

Internet Explorer has an automatic **Pop-up blocker**, lets you surf the Web **InPrivate** and has a **SmartScreen Filter** to help keep you safe and your online data secure.

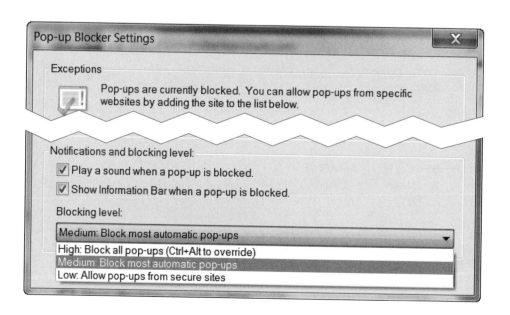

Deal with pop-up messages that state your computer isn't secure, has a virus, or isn't performing to its potential

Do pop-up messages occasionally appear on your computer stating that you don't have anti-virus software installed, that Microsoft has detected problems with your computer and may have solutions, that you aren't protected from malware, or something similar?

You may see pop-ups when you're online too, stating that you need to run a Registry check, that you *have* a virus or malware, or that you need to download and install a specific program to fix problems with your computer.

Unless you're quite savvy about computers and how they work, these messages can be confusing. Have you heard the stories about people that click on these kinds of messages, who install a Registry "cleaner" or some such thing, and end up with a virus or malware because of it? Which security messages are real and which are fake?

First, it's important to understand that when you're online and visiting websites, any pop-ups that appear during your online sessions are probably *not* from Microsoft. When you're online and a pop-up appears stating that your Registry needs to be cleaned or that you have a virus, ***don't fall for it***; Windows 7 gives you a way to determine if you really do have problems like these.

Second, if a pop-up appears in the bottom right corner of your Desktop that really *does* look legitimate, again, there's a way to find out if it is.

Which websites have you visited that resulted in pop-ups appearing, even when Internet Explorer's Pop-up Blocker is enabled? Do specific types of websites seem to be worse than others?

Find and resolve problems with the Action Center

When you see an error message about a security problem, a maintenance problem, or even a message that states resolutions have been found for problems previously discovered, what do you do? Unless you're positive it's a message from the Windows 7 Action Center, *you shouldn't click it*.

But what if you see a pop-up message that you're sure is legitimate and from Windows 7, but it disappears before you can click it? What then? Can you access that message once it's pulled a vanishing act?

To find those vanishing messages and find out if you really *do* have problems, if there really are security issues, or if solutions really have been found, open the Action Center manually.

Type Action Center in the Start Search window, and click **Action Center** from the results, or open the Action Center from the Taskbar. Just click the Action Center icon on the Taskbar's Notification Area, then choose **Open Action Center**.

Once inside the **Action Center** you'll see any problems that currently exist, and the options for resolving them. The solutions provided are generally self-explanatory. You may need to get anti-virus software, you may be prompted that a problematic driver now has an update, or you may be prompted to turn on Windows Defender, Windows Firewall, or Windows Update, for example.

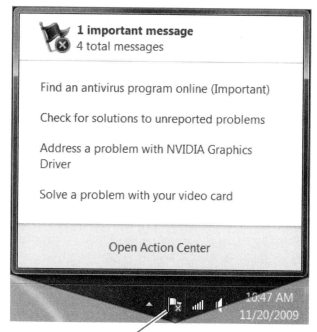

The Action Center icon is available in the Taskbar's Notification area.

When a problem is listed, click **Check for solutions**, **View message details**, or in the case of anti-virus software, **Find a program online**. Note that you can also turn off certain notifications, as with the notifications regarding anti-virus software.

Depending on the problem, Action Center will offer steps to resolve the issue. You may even get the option to have Windows check for solutions regarding unreported problems. You may be given the option to go to a website to download a new driver. Your objective is to resolve all of the problems in the Action Center.

Play with it

Open the Action Center and you'll see error messages, warnings, or suggestions to make your computer more secure or to make it perform better. If there's a driver to install, go ahead and install it. If you have an anti-virus program installed but Windows doesn't recognize it, click the option to stop sending you notifications about it. If you see an option to have Windows check for solutions to problems it has previously found, do that too.

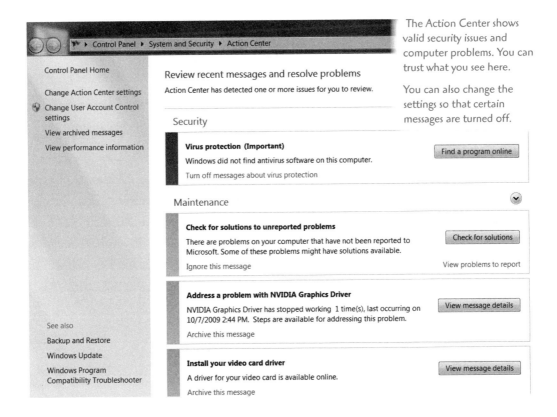

The Action Center shows valid security issues and computer problems. You can trust what you see here.

You can also change the settings so that certain messages are turned off.

What problems did you find while inside the Action Center? What did you do to resolve them?

Do you have a problem because you have no anti-virus software? Maybe you didn't want to purchase it. There's a solution for that! Check out Microsoft Security Essentials at www.microsoft.com/Security_Essentials/. Click Download, follow the simple instructions, and you'll be covered.

Find and resolve problems using Windows Defender

But what about pop-ups that aren't from Internet Explorer or the Action Center, what can you do about those? Unscrupulous websites can cause pop-up messages to appear on your PC stating that you have a virus, that you have a Registry problem, or that you need to install specific software to keep your computer safe.

It's all too easy to fall for these messages, believe they come from Microsoft, and click the message. If you do, a virus, malware, or spyware *could be* installed. The problem is that there is nothing wrong with your computer; the message is only a ploy to get you to install something you don't want or need, or worse, cause damage to your computer or compromise your personal data.

If you receive a message stating that your computer has a virus and it's not from your anti-virus program or Windows Defender, **stop!** *Don't click anything*! Instead, open **Windows Defender**, run a scan, and see what Windows has to say about it. (If you don't get anywhere with that, run a scan using your own anti-virus software.)

But what is **Windows Defender**? It's okay, you can trust it. It's a program that runs quietly in the background of Windows 7, protecting your computer from spyware and malware, and even unwanted software. The best way to open Windows Defender is to search for it in the Start menu.

Once Windows Defender is open, you can tell immediately if there's a problem with your PC. Here's a healthy PC. You can run a scan if you want to, just to be sure. Scans run daily, though, generally in the middle of the night.

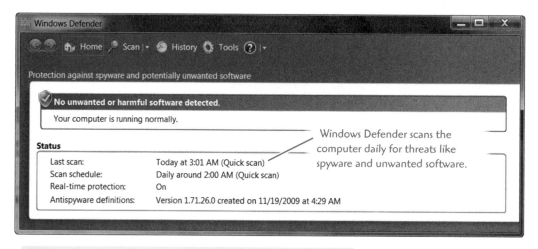

Windows Defender scans the computer daily for threats like spyware and unwanted software.

Click **Tools** in Windows Defender to see additional settings. There's one item in particular you should check out and that's **Options**. Under Options are settings you can change to define how often and when to perform scans, how to respond to threats found, what to scan (like downloaded files and attachments), and whether or not to scan e-mail, removable drives, and create restore points. Although the defaults are fine, it never hurts to have a look.

Tools and Settings

Settings ———————————————————

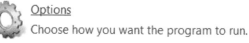

Options
Choose how you want the program to run.

Secure your computer with Windows Update

Windows Update is an application you're already familiar with. Windows Update is set up to check for updates automatically, but it's a good idea to check on Windows Update occasionally for yourself. From Windows Update you can:

→ View and install optional updates.

→ Install important updates.

→ Check for updates manually.

→ Change settings for Windows Update.

Visit **Windows Update** now, click **Start > All Programs > Windows Update**. What do you see? If there are updates to view or install, do that now.

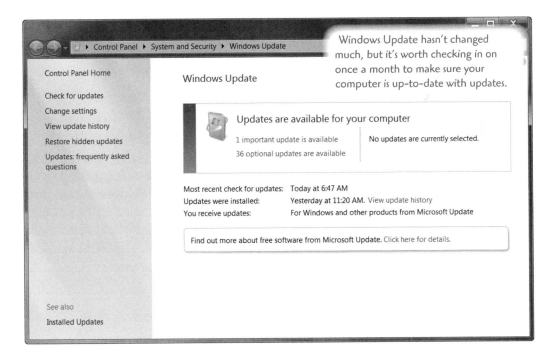

Did you find any updates that were not installed while you were in the Windows Update window? Did you manually get updates? What happened?

Play with it

Is Windows Update configured to install updates automatically? Windows Update should be configured to download and install updates automatically for best results. To find out if your computer is configured to do this, open Windows Update, and click **Change Settings**.

Although you can configure the settings any way you like, the following settings are recommended:

→ Install updates automatically.

→ Install updates every day at a time when the computer is idle and connected to the Internet.

→ Install recommended updates and allow all users to install updates.

→ Install updates for Microsoft products and check for updates periodically.

Maintain your computer

If you don't maintain your car with regular oil changes, the car can develop engine problems. If you don't maintain your body with good food and regular exercise, your body can develop health problems. If you don't maintain your computer, do you think it could develop problems?

But what do you need to do and how often? You already know some things about maintaining your PC; write down your ideas here:

Did you write down "Use Disk Cleanup once a month"? How about "Uninstall unnecessary programs and data a few times a year"? What about "Clean up Internet Explorer"?

Those are all very important things to do regularly, but you can do more. "Regularly" is a relative term though, completely related to how much data you have. The idea is to keep the clutter to a minimum by keeping unwanted data off your PC, performing tasks to keep the computer physically clean and safe, and running maintenance routines, like Disk Cleanup.

Here are some ideas:

☐ Keep your anti-virus software up-to-date. Get updated definitions daily if possible.

☐ Perform regular backups. Back up important data as it is created. Create regular weekly backups.

☐ Have some sort of backup system in place. You may copy important data to a flash drive, burn CDs or DVDs, or use the Backup and Restore program that comes with Windows 7. You may also opt to store data online at places like **Box.net** or Windows Office Workspace. For the best protection possible, incorporate more than one of these options.

☐ Use Disk Cleanup four to six times a year.

This removes temporary Internet files (which cause Internet Explorer to run slowly when there are too many); empties the Recycle Bin (which frees up hard drive space), removes downloaded installation files (once a program is installed, installation files are no longer needed); set up log files (these are files that are created during set-up for troubleshooting should set-up go bad); compress old files (frees up hard drive space by compressing rarely used files).

☐ Make sure that Disk Defragmenter is scheduled to defragment your disks automatically. Windows 7 should automatically configure Disk Defragmenter to run once a week, but it's always good to double check.

☐ Uninstall programs you don't use using the Control Panel. (Don't just delete program folders.)

Installed and unwanted programs take up hard drive space. Some run in the background all the time using up system resources (like QuickTime, and some music programs), and many programs in Control Panel are "trials" that come with a new PC.

☐ In your e-mail program, first delete all the e-mail in your Sent folder, then delete e-mail you no longer need, and finally delete the items in your Deleted Items folder. Do this three times a year or more.

☐ If you have a desktop PC, open the case and use canned air to blow out the dust that's accumulated. Do this twice a year, *being careful not to touch anything in the case with the can or your hands.*

> A computer will crash if too much dust accumulates inside the case—you'll even get memory errors if there's dust on the memory chips.

☐ Use surge protectors and consider a Uninterruptible Power Supply (UPS) device in case the power goes out.

> A bad surge can ruin a good PC and make it useless.

☐ Restart your PC at least once a week. And although there are various schools of thought, turn your PC off for a while every now and then to give it a "break."

> Restarting gives the PC a fresh start.

☐ Verify safeguards are enabled set to their default settings: Disk Defragmenter, System Restore, Windows Update, etc.

☐ Do not install programs that are controversial such as Kazaa, LimeWire, or other "sharing" programs.

> These programs can introduce viruses to your PC.

☐ Twice a year, at the Run line, type `sfc /scannow`. This will scan for missing system files and replace them.

> Click Start, and type Run in the Start Search window.
> Click Run in the results list.

☐ If you can't afford anti-virus or spyware protection, consider free alternatives like Ad-Aware or Microsoft's Security Essentials.

☐ Create a system restore disc. Go to Start > All Programs > Maintenance > Create a System Repair Disc to get started.

Take a break

That's it—which means it's time to take a break. You need to give your brain some down time away from the new material. Just make sure to come back to do the Review and Experiment. They provide a great means to solidify the content in your brain.

Review

↺ Based on your personal experience, which of the following are valid pop-ups with legitimate warnings?

☐ Notifications from the Action Center regarding security issues like having no anti-virus software installed.

☐ Notifications while at a website that warns you that your computer is infected by a virus.

☐ Notifications from Windows Updates that updates were installed or are ready for installation.

☐ Warnings that there is something wrong with the computer's Registry, and that you should run a Registry cleaning program.

☐ Notifications in the Notification Area of the Taskbar stating solutions to current problems have been found.

↺ The Action Center is part of Windows 7 and offers a list of potential problems and their solutions. Problems can include: ....
and ....

↺ Windows Defender scans daily for .... and ....

↺ Name the other three of the five things Windows Update offers:

1. Optional Updates.

2. ....

3. ....

4. ....

5. The option to check for updates manually.

Continues, flip the page

○ Internet Explorer offers two new features to help you stay safe online: .... and .... To tell Internet Explorer to not make a note of the websites you've visited, save cookies, or maintain temporary Internet files for future reference, start an .... session. To report a website as unsafe, use the .... Filter.

○ Name seven things you can do to maintain your PC:

1. ....

2. ....

3. ....

4. ....

5. ....

6. ....

7. ....

How did you do?

Did you forget anything? It's hard to remember it all. Go ahead and re-read the sections covering what you overlooked. Your brain might need a bit more time to absorb all the information.

Experiment

The best way to really cement these features and techniques into your long-term memory is to expand on the techniques you just learned about by using them and taking them just one step further.

Here are some suggestions for your experiment using techniques covered in this chapter.

Know your Windows Experience Index and learn what you can do to improve performance

The **Windows Experience Index** tells you quite a bit about your computer and how well it can and should perform. In turn, that information will help you find out how you can improve your computer performance.

To find your Experience Index, click Start and right-click Computer then choose Properties. Your computer's rating will appear in the System properties window. Click **Windows Experience Index**, in blue, to find out more.

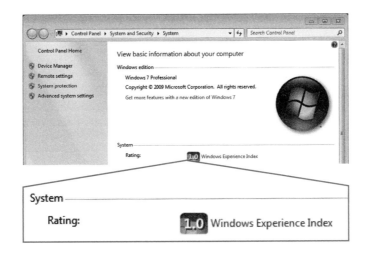

You can use this information to find the "weakest link." For instance, if Memory (RAM) has the lowest subscore of all of the available rated components, you can add memory to increase performance.

Speaking of improving performance, did you know you can now add RAM externally using a USB flash drive? You can, and the technology behind it is called **ReadyBoost**. If you have a flash drive handy, insert it now. When prompted, select to use the drive as additional RAM.

Index

A

Accelerators, 46, 50–53, 54, 55
access point (wireless access point), 18, 200
accounts. *See* e-mail accounts; user accounts
Action Center, 211–213, 219
Ad-Aware, 218
Add or Change Home Page dialog box, 45
Add or Remove User Accounts, 159, 168, 169, 204
Add to calendar option, 37–39
adjust color option, 73
adjust detail option, 73
adjust exposure option, 73
Administrator account, 157, 168–170
Aero feature. *See* Peek; Shake; Snap
All Accelerators option, 52, 55
All Programs menu, 4, 6, 7, 12, 100
alphabetical sorting (icons), 5
Alt key, 26, 28, 32, 42, 43
Alt + P, 135
anti-virus programs, 207, 211, 212, 213, 214, 217, 218, 219
Arrange by Dates (photos/pictures), 67
arrow (next to Home button), 45
authentication requirements, 25
auto adjust (Live Photo Gallery), 68
automatic connection (to networks), 132–133
Automatic Sync, 85
auto playlist (Create auto playlist command), 85
AutoPlay settings, 136–137, 141

B

Back to gallery button, 64, 69
Backup and Restore program, 217
backups, 22, 57, 63, 92, 143, 150, 180, 207, 217
Bing Maps, 53
black and white effects, 73
BlackBerries, 62
blogs, 22, 44, 55, 70

B

BookCrossing folder, 145, 146, 147, 148, 150, 151, 181
broken web pages, 50
Burn a DVD (Live Photo Gallery), 72
Burn tab (Media Player), 85, 101

C

Calendar feature (Live Mail), 37–39
canned air, 218
Change Desktop Items, 4
Choose Details dialog box, 153
Colorizer button, 33
Command Bar, 32, 33, 43, 44
Compatibility button (Internet Explorer), 50
computer maintenance checklist, 216–218. *See also* maintenance
connectivity options (networks), 16–20, 132–133
Contacts icon (Live Mail), 30, 31
copying/moving
    data, to Public Folders, 178–179
    documents, 124
    media files, 92
    music, to PCs, 76, 77, 92
    photos/pictures, 63, 66, 92
Create autoplaylist, 85
Create playlist, 85, 89
cropping photos, 68
Ctrl, 28
Ctrl + P, 135
Ctrl + T, 45
Ctrl + X, 135
Cut command, 63

D

Delete button (Live Mail), 30, 31
Desktop background pictures, 66, 67
Desktop enhancement features, 1–13
Desktop Gadget Gallery, 6, 7, 100
dialog boxes

Add or Change Home Page, 45
Choose Details, 153
Documents Properties, 146
File Sharing, 193
Internet Options, 42, 43, 54, 208
Manage Accounts, 160
Print, 135
Run, 27
Taskbar and Start Menu Properties, 131
digital cameras, 61–62
Digital Living Network Alliance (DLNA)
    compliant device, 82
disabling
    notifications, 130–131
    Password Protected Sharing, 167
    Peek, 131
    Snap, 133
    UAC, 134
Disk Cleanup, 217
Disk Defragmenter, 217, 218
display resolution, 2, 111
DLNA (Digital Living Network Alliance)
    compliant device, 82
documents (copying/moving documents), 124
Documents Library, 124, 143, 146, 147, 150,
    152, 194
Documents Properties dialog box, 146
downloading
    Live Mail, 21
    Live Photo Gallery, 59
DVD Maker, 72
DVDs, Media Center/Media Player and, 102

E

Edit (Menu Bar), 32, 33, 42, 44
e-mail
    junk e-mail options, 30, 31, 34, 35
    spam, 22, 23, 34
    Unread e-mail option, 29
e-mail accounts, 24–28
e-mail programs. *See also* **Live Mail**
    Gmail, 23
    Hotmail, 22, 23, 55, 198
    Outlook, 15, 23, 25, 30, 35, 161, 218
    Outlook Express, 15, 23, 24, 26, 28, 30, 32,
        33, 35
    Windows Mail, 23, 26, 28, 32, 35

Yahoo! Plus, 23
Ethernet networks, 16–17
Event Album (Publish › Event Album), 70
Explorer bars, 42
exporting. *See* importing
extenders. *See* media extenders

F

Facebook, 22, 41, 44, 50, 55, 70
Favorites Bar
    Menu Bar and, 32, 42
    Suggested Sites, 44
    Web Slices, 46–47, 54
Favorites list (Media Center TV), 121
Feeds, 30, 31, 42
File and Printer Sharing, 156, 167, 175, 182,
    189
File Sharing dialog box, 193
file types/extensions, 136–137
filtering. *See also* **sort options**
    junk e-mail, 30, 31, 34, 35
    SmartScreen Filter, 208, 209, 210
    Start Search results, 125–127
Find More Providers option, 48
Flickr, 22, 70
Folder Options, 140
folders. *See* Libraries; Public Folders; *specific*
    folders
Format button, 37
Forward button, 30
full-screen mode, 80, 111, 116

G

gadgets, 6–7
    Desktop Gadget Gallery, 6, 7, 100
    Media Center Desktop Gadget, 100
    Peek and, 10, 46
    sidebar and, 6
    Weather, 6, 7, 10
    Web Slices *v.*, 46
    Win+G shortcut, 135
Gmail, 23
Group Album (Publish › Group Album), 70
Guest account, 157, 163–164

H

Happy Hour example, 50, 52, 53

hard drive
    computer maintenance checklist, 216–218
    sharing data on, 182–184
    space, 114–115
Help (Menu Bar), 33, 42
Help and Support, 8, 127
History
    delete, 44, 54
    Explorer bar, 42
Home (network type), 16, 17, 18
Home button, arrow and, 45
HomeGroup, 189–205
    creating, 191
    folder sharing (with one person), 205
    joining, 190, 192
    network/sharing fixes, 200–201
    permissions, 192–193
    personalization, 194–199
    Play to option and, 75, 82
Hotmail, 22, 23, 55, 198
hotspots, 19
hovering cursor
    Calendar feature and, 39
    Media Player playback modes and, 83–84
    over Bing Maps, 53
    over bottom of Media Center screen, 112
    over Gadgets, 7
    over Peek spot, 10, 131
    over photos/pictures, 66
    over Taskbar icons, 83–84, 128

I

icons (on Desktop), 4–5. *See also specific icons*
ieaddons.com, 47
images. *See* photos/pictures
importing
    e-mail accounts/messages, 26–28
    import/export option (File-Menu Bar), 44
    photos/pictures, 59–63, 92
inline spell check feature, 36
InPrivate Browsing, 208–209, 210
installation
    digital camera, 62
    Internet TV installation tasks, 118, 119
    Live ID Sign-in Assistant, 198
    Live Mail, 21, 35
    Live Photo Gallery, 59

TV tuner, 109
    uninstall programs (Control Panel), 217
Internet Explorer 8, 41–55
    Compatibility button, 50
    Favorites Bar. *See* Favorites Bar
    ieaddons.com, 47
    InPrivate Browsing, 208–209, 210
    Menu Bar. *See* Menu Bar
    Pop-up Blocker settings, 209–210, 211
    safety features, 208–210
    search options, 48–49
    SmartScreen Filter, 208, 209, 210
    tabbed browsing, 44–45, 54
    Web Slices, 46–47, 54
Internet Options dialog box, 42, 43, 54, 208
Internet Service Providers. *See* ISPs
Internet TV, 118–119
iPhones, 62, 84, 141
ISPs (Internet Service Providers), 15, 23, 24, 218
iTunes, 62, 75, 76, 84, 91, 132, 136, 141, 160, 163, 175

J

Jump Lists, 83, 88, 129
junk e-mail options, 30, 31, 34, 35

K

keyboard shortcuts. *See* shortcuts

L

Layout (Menus icon/button), 33
libraries (Media Center libraries), 96–98
Libraries (Windows Libraries), 143–153
    creating, 148–151, 181
    Documents Library, 124, 143, 146, 147, 150, 152, 194
    Music Library, 77, 78, 85, 87, 94, 95, 98, 143
    Pictures Library, 63, 66, 67, 146, 153, 179, 196
    Public, 179, 181
    searching inside, 149–150
    Videos Library, 144–145
    Views, 153
linked online ID, 198–199, 204, 205
Live Call, 22
Live Essentials (Windows Live Essentials), 21,

57, 71
Live ID (Windows Live ID), 22
  blogging and, 55
  as e-mail account, 23–24
  linked, 198–199, 204, 205
  Live ID Sign-in Assistant, 198
Live Mail (Windows Live Mail), 15–39
  downloading, 21
  features/options, 30–34
  setting up, 23–29
Live Messenger (Windows Live Messenger), 15, 21, 22, 35, 38, 129
Live Photo Gallery (Windows Live Photo Gallery), 57–73. *See also* **photos/pictures**
  Back to gallery button, 64, 69
  downloading, 59
  DVD Maker and, 72
  features, 57
Live Toolbar (Windows Live Toolbar), 15, 22, 35
Live Web Page, 69–70
Live Writer (Windows Live Writer), 35, 70
Log Off option, 162

M

Mail. *See* **Live Mail; Windows Mail**
maintenance, 207–221
  checklist (for computers), 216–218
  Internet Explorer safety features, 208–210
  TV recordings and, 114–115
malware, 156, 163, 207, 211, 214
Manage Accelerators option, 55
Manage Accounts dialog box, 160
Manage Libraries, 78, 92
Manage Search Providers option, 48
Manage wireless networks, 132
media cards
  importing media from, 60, 61, 92
  password reset disk and, 173
Media Center (Windows Media Center), 91–105
  Media Player v., 91–105
  new features, 98–100, 103
  TV options, 107–121. *See also* TV options
media extenders, 100, 103, 104, 105, 107, 194
media files, 92, 98. *See also* **music access options; photos/pictures; streaming media; TV options; videos**
Media Player (Windows Media Player), 75–89
  Media Center v., 91–105
  MP3 player sync with, 84–85
  music access (on other PCs) with, 76–82
  music playing with, 83–84
  new features, 103
  playback modes (from Taskbar), 83–84
  videos and, 93–94
  visualizations, 86–87, 101
media sharing (enabled), 78, 79, 82
Media Streaming option, 167, 185
Menu Bar (Internet Explorer), 42–43
  Alt key, 26, 28, 32, 42, 43
  Edit, 32, 33, 42, 44
  File, 44
  Help, 33, 42
  History, 42
  Show Menu Bar, 33, 42–43
  show permanently, 43
  Tools, 26, 33, 42, 43, 54, 208
Menus icon/button, 30, 31, 33, 36, 38
  inline spell check feature, 36
  Layout, 33
  Options, 30
  Safety Options, 34
  Show Menu Bar, 33
Messenger. *See* **Live Messenger**
Microsoft Office Outlook, 15, 23, 25, 30, 35, 161, 218
Microsoft's Security Essentials, 218
minimizing
  windows (Shake), 7–9. *See also* Peek
  Windows Media Player, 83
mixed network (sharing data over mixed network), 175–187
mouse cursor. *See* **hovering cursor**
moving. *See* **copying/moving**
MP3 players, sync option for, 84–85
multiple web pages (tabbed browsing), 44–45, 54
multiple windows. *See* **windows**
Multiply, 70
music access options (accessing music on other PCs), 76–82
music copying, 76, 77, 92
Music Library, 77, 78, 85, 87, 94, 95, 98, 143

MySpace, 44

N

Navigation pane, 67, 93, 96
network access point, 18, 200
Network and Sharing Center, 17, 19, 20,
   166–167
Network Discovery, 17, 19, 20, 167
network folders, 64, 92, 143
Network icon, 17, 18, 19, 20, 177, 190
networks. *See also* **sharing data; social
   networking sites**
   connectivity options, 16–20, 132–133
   mixed, 175–187
   music access over, 76, 78–80
   photo access over, 64
   Public, 16, 17, 18
   wireless, 18–19, 132
   Work, 16, 17, 18
New button (Live Mail), 30
New library option, 148
Newsgroups icon (Live Mail), 30, 31
Notification Area, 127. *See also* **Peek**
   Action Center, 211–213, 219
   disabling notifications, 130–131
   Network icon, 17, 18, 19, 20, 177, 190
Now Playing view, 80, 86, 87

O

Office Live Workspace, 187
Office Outlook, 15, 23, 25, 30, 35, 161, 218
online ID. *See* **Live ID**
online storage (Live ID), 22
openwifispots.com, 19
Options
   Menus icon/button, 30, 36
   Tools and, 26
   Windows Defender, 214
Outlook (Microsoft Office Outlook), 15, 23,
   25, 30, 35, 161, 218
Outlook Express, 15, 23, 24, 26, 28, 30, 32,
   33, 35

P

Page (Command Bar), 44
panoramic photos, 70, 72
Parental Controls option, 164–165
Password Protected Sharing, 167, 172, 176,
   177, 182
password-protected Standard user accounts,
   157–160, 168–170
password reset disk, 173
Paste command, 27, 50, 63, 67
Peek, 7, 10–11, 46, 131
performance (Windows Experience Index),
   207, 221
personalization
   gadgets, 7
   HomeGroup, 194–199
   shortcuts/personalization options, 133–141
Personalization window, 2–3
   Change Desktop Items, 4
   options, 2–3
   sound schemes, 13
Personal Storage Table (PST), 218
phishing, 207, 209
Photobucket, 22
photos/pictures (Live Photo Gallery), 57–73.
   See also **Live Photo Gallery**
   accessed over network, 64–65
   adjust color option, 73
   adjust detail option, 73
   adjust exposure option, 73
   Arrange by Dates option, 67
   auto adjust, 68
   black and white effects, 73
   copying/moving, 63, 66, 92
   cropping, 68
   as Desktop background, 66, 67
   editing options, 68–69, 73
   hovering cursor over, 66
   importing, 59–63, 92
   organizing, 66–67
   panoramic, 70, 72
   publishing, 69–70
   rating, 65, 66
   red eye in, 68
   resizing, 66
   rotating, 66, 67
   sharing, 69–70, 72–73
   slideshows, 60, 72, 101, 104
   straightening, 68
   thumbnail options, 65
Photo Wall feature, 99–100, 103
pictures. *See* **photos/pictures**

Pictures Library, 63, 66, 67, 146, 153, 179, 196
Pin to Taskbar, 128–129
playlists (Create playlist/autoplaylist), 85, 89
Play Pictures, 99
Play to option, 75, 82
POP3 server, 24, 25
Pop-up Blocker settings, 209–210, 211
pop-up messages, 209–214
port requirements, 25
PowerPoint, 60, 129
Print dialog box, 135
printer sharing (File and Printer Sharing), 156, 167, 175, 182, 189
program shortcuts, 4, 12
PST (Personal Storage Table), 218
Public (network type), 16, 17, 18
Public Documents folder, 147, 180
Public Folders, 176–182, 185
Public Folders Sharing, 150, 156, 167, 175, 176, 177, 182
Public Library, 179, 181
Public Videos folder, 145, 180
Publish › Event Album, 70
Publish › Group Album, 70
publishing photos, 69–70
Publish › More Services, 70

Q
Quick Launch toolbar, 127, 128
Quick Views, 29

R
rating (photos/pictures), 65, 66
recording (TV recording), 112–116
red eye, 68
Registry warnings (malware messages), 211, 213, 219
Remote Media Streaming, 76, 80–81
remove user accounts (Add or Remove User Accounts), 159, 168, 169, 204
Reply all button, 30
Reply button, 30
resizing
    icons, 5
    photos/pictures, 66
Rip command, 85

rotating pictures, 66, 67
Run dialog box, 27

S
safety. *See also* **security**
    Internet Explorer, 208–210
    Safety option (Command Bar), 44
    Safety Options (Menus icon), 34
    Standard user accounts, 158
    User Accounts and Family Safety, 164, 173
Save Search feature, 140–141
screen resolution, 2, 111
screen savers
    through Live Photo Gallery, 69
    in Personalization window, 2, 3
search options
    advanced, 140–141
    inside Libraries, 149–150
    Internet Explorer, 48–49
    Save Search feature, 140–141
    Start Search feature, 124–127, 140
second monitor, 121
secret features (Accelerator icon), 51
security. *See also* safety
    Action Center, 211–213, 219
    Microsoft's Security Essentials, 213
    pop-up messages and, 209–214
    user accounts and, 155–173
    Windows Defender, 212, 213–214, 219
Security Essentials (Microsoft), 218
Security tab (Internet Options dialog box), 43
Send/Receive button, 32
Send To (command), 4, 12
set as Desktop background (pictures), 66, 67
Shake, 7–9
Share personal folders with › HomeGroup, 197, 199
Share with › linked online ID, 198–199, 204, 205
Share with › Nobody, 196, 197, 199
sharing data. *See also* HomeGroup; networks; Public Folders
    on hard drive, 182–184
    HomeGroup and, 189–205
    Office Live Workspace and, 187
    over mixed network, 175–187
    photos/pictures, 69–70, 72–73

Switch User option, 161–162
shortcuts
   keyboard shortcuts, 28, 45, 135
   personalization/shortcuts options, 123–141
   program shortcuts, 4, 12
Show Menu Bar, 33, 42–43
Show on Desktop, 4
sidebar, 6. *See also* **gadgets**
side-by-side comparisons
   Media Player/ Media Center, 102–103
   Photo Gallery/Windows Explorer window, 65
   windows (Snap), 7, 9–10
sizing icons, 5
skins (Media Player), 86
Slide Show Maker, 100, 103
slideshows, 60, 72, 101, 104
SmartScreen Filter, 208, 209, 210
SMTP server, 24, 25
Snap, 7, 9–10, 133
social networking sites, 22, 60, 70
   Facebook, 22, 41, 44, 50, 55, 70
   Flickr, 22, 70
   Multiply, 70
   MySpace, 44
   Photobucket, 22
   Twitter, 22, 44, 55
   Wordpress, 22
   YouTube, 70
Sort by menu, 5
sort options
   Details view (Libraries), 153
   Details view (Start Search), 126
   folder data (Live Mail), 35
   folder data (Live Photo Gallery), 66
   icons, 5
spam, 22, 23, 34
Spelling tab, 36
spyware, 207, 214, 218
Standard user accounts, 157–160, 168–170
Start Search feature, 124–127, 140
Stationery option, 37
storage online (Live ID), 22
Store folder, 26, 27
straighten photo (Live Photo Gallery), 68
streaming media, 81, 101
   HomeGroup and, 194–195
   Media Streaming option, 167, 185

Remote Media Streaming, 76, 80–81
   Stream media with devices option, 194
   Stream menu, 78, 81
subfolders, 63, 67, 71, 144, 147, 149, 150, 179
surfing the Internet. *See* **Internet Explorer**
surge protectors, 218
Switch User option, 161–162
synchronization
   Automatic Sync option, 85
   Live ID and, 22
   MP3 players/Media Player, 84–85
   Sync button (Live Mail), 29, 32
System Restore, 218

T

tabbed browsing (tabs), 44–45, 54
tabs. *See* **tabbed browsing**
Taskbar, 127–131. *See also* **Notification Area**
   Jump Lists on, 83, 88, 129
   Media Player playback modes from, 83–84
Taskbar and Start Menu Properties dialog box,
   131
television. *See* **TV options**
third-party program's proprietary folder, 149
thumbnails, 65, 128, 138
Tools
   on Command Bar, 43, 44
   on Menu Bar, 26, 33, 42, 43, 54, 208
tuner (TV tuner), 108–110
Turbo Scroll, 98, 103
TV options (Media Center), 107–121
   Favorites list, 121
   hard drive space and, 114–115
   Internet TV, 118–119
   Media Center v. Media Player, 103
   recording options, 112–116
   second monitor, 121
   tuner, 108–110
   TV picture improvement, 111
Twitter, 22, 44, 55

U

UAC (User Account Control), 134, 139, 157,
   170
uninstall programs (Control Panel), 217
Uninterruptible Power Supply (UPS), 218
Unread e-mail option, 29

Unread from contacts option, 29
updates (Windows Update), 215–216
UPS (Uninterruptible Power Supply), 218
USB flash drives, 27, 143, 151, 152, 153, 221.
    See also media cards
user accounts, 155–173
    Add or Remove User Accounts, 159, 168, 169,
        204
    Administrator account, 157, 168–170
    Guest account, 157, 163–164
    Live ID linked with, 198–199, 204, 205
    password-protected Standard user accounts,
        157–160, 168–170
    UAC, 134, 139, 157, 170
    User Accounts and Family Safety, 164, 173

V
videos, 92–96, 102
Videos Library, 144–145
View menu (Media Player), 86
Views (Library Views), 153
viruses, 163, 211, 212, 213, 214, 217, 218,
    219
visualizations, 86–87, 101

W
Weather gadget, 6, 7, 10
web pages
    broken, 50
    multiple (tabbed browsing), 44–45, 54
website-specific searches, 48
Web Slices, 46–47, 54
"Wildlife in HD" video, 93, 95
windows
    minimizing, 7–9
    Peek, 7, 10–11
    Shake, 7–9
    side-by-side, 7, 9–10
    Snap, 7, 9–10
Windows Defender, 212, 213–214, 219
Windows DVD Maker, 72
Windows Experience Index, 207, 221
Windows Explorer
    HomeGroup computers and, 192
    Jump List, 129
    Live Photo Gallery v., 65
Windows Libraries. *See* Libraries

Windows Live Essentials. *See* Live Essentials
Windows Mail, 23, 26, 28, 32, 35. *See also* Live
    Mail
Windows Media Center. *See* Media Center
Windows Media Player. *See* Media Player
Windows Update, 215–216
wireless access point, 18, 200
wireless network icon, 18
wireless networks, 18–19, 132
Wordpress, 22
Work (network type), 16, 17, 18

X
Xbox 360, 100, 103, 105, 107, 194
Xbox Live, 22

Y
Yahoo! Plus, 23
yellow star, 44
YouTube, 70

Z
Zune, 62, 75, 76, 84